The Snow Globe Effect

An 8-week Mindfulness Program for Leaders

Lydia Richards
Al Polito

Books may be purchased by contacting the publisher and author at: CreateSpace, a DBA of On-Demand Publishing, LLC, a division of Amazon

FIRST EDITION

Library of Congress Cataloging-in-Publication Data

Names: Lydia Richards, Al Polito, Aerowenn Hunter
Title: The Snow Globe Effect: An 8-Week Mindfulness Program for Leaders
Design: Teddi Jensen Design
Description: First Edition
Publisher: Teamworks
Identifiers: ISBN: 978-0-9997493-0-2

Subjects: LCSH: Meditation, Mindfulness. Happiness
BISAC: SELF-HELP Personal Growth, Happiness, Leadership
BODY, MIND, & SPIRIT / Meditation, Leadership

Printed in the United States of America

Table of Contents

Preface 6

The Snow Globe Effect.................... 8

Understanding Mindfulness 12

Mindfulness and Leadership 22

Emotional Intelligence 24

Cultivating Mindfulness 30

The Program 34

Week 1: *Noticing Your Attention* 50

Week 2: *Quieting the Chatter* 60

Week 3: *Outsmarting Your Brain* 66

Week 4: *Living in Gratitude* 80

Week 5: *Accepting What Is*................ 92

Week 6: *Choosing Happiness* 100

Week 7: *Find Your Fire*...................110

Week 8: *Moving Beyond our Stories* 120

Final Thoughts 132

The quality of your mind **determines the quality of your leadership**

...and your life.

This book is not about leadership.
It's about the leader

...you!

Preface

Stephen, the manager of a large division of an international corporation, was kind, likeable, funny, and smart. A quick scan of the dozens of books on leadership in his office showed just how much he wanted to be a great leader. No doubt he could have quoted *Good to Great* by chapter and verse.

However, far from being great, Stephen was failing in leadership. His employees were disgruntled, little was being accomplished well, tensions were running high, he was frustrated and bewildered.

Stephen is not alone.

Current research on leadership indicates, "53% of leaders are generating demotivating working climates. And only 25% of HR professionals globally view their organization's leadership as high quality."[1]

Surely, many of those who are generating toxic workplaces are like Stephen—smart, well-meaning people who want to be effective leaders.

In terms of leadership, something was obviously missing for Stephen.

What was missing?

For years, I poured everything I knew into teaching leadership within corporations. I taught senior executives, middle managers, and frontline supervisors how to inspire, motivate, and engage their people. Participants in our leadership development programs returned to their companies better-informed and empowered to lead. However, when it came to implementing the lessons they had learned, the results were often disappointing. For some reason, great learning wasn't translating into great leading.

Something was still missing.

To get to the bottom of it, I dissected our participants' experiences and picked over conversations, meetings, annual reviews, and informal interactions. A new picture began to emerge into my own personal "a-ha" moment. From that knowing, this book was born.

The *something* that Stephen and many others like him are missing is a settled mind, a mind that sees things clearly, accepts situations as they are, and is free to respond with insight and compassion.

That something is

mindfulness.

Your mind is like a snow globe.

When you shake a snow globe, the snow swirls and the beautiful image within is lost.

The same thing occurs within our minds. When we are agitated, it's hard to see life clearly. Stress, distraction, and crazy-busy lives shake up the snow globe of the mind, creating continuous flurries. Seeing clearly is impossible.

But when we set the snow globe down, the snow gently settles on its own. Everything becomes peaceful and clear. Likewise, as we take time to breathe, quiet the mind, and observe our own experience, our minds naturally settle, and we begin to see ourselves and the world around us with greater clarity. We become more self-aware, open to possibilities, responsive, and able to think more expansively.

The Snow Globe Effect

With a settled mind, people tend to make better decisions, focus their attention, solve problems more creatively, and remain calm and peaceful even in the midst of chaos. They are far more resilient. When the mind settles, deep states of relaxation, contentment, and happiness naturally emerge.

This program is designed to help you, the leader,

settle your mind.

A review of best-selling books, articles, and studies on leadership shows considerable agreement. In order to be a brilliant leader (or even just a good one) there is a short list of must-have abilities that need to be mastered—in other words, diligently working on this list will cause you to become a great leader.

But the reality is that if you approach this list as abilities that must be mastered one by one, you will be wasting a lot of energy and your results will be uneven at best. Such a list should rather be viewed as the effect, rather than the cause, of a good leader.

Therein lies a potential problem: if your mind is agitated and unsettled, no amount of "leadership development" will be able to transform you into an effective leader. Without the foundation of a settled mind, you will be unable to see some things clearly and to respond with insight and compassion.

There is a more productive and effective way to become a great leader:

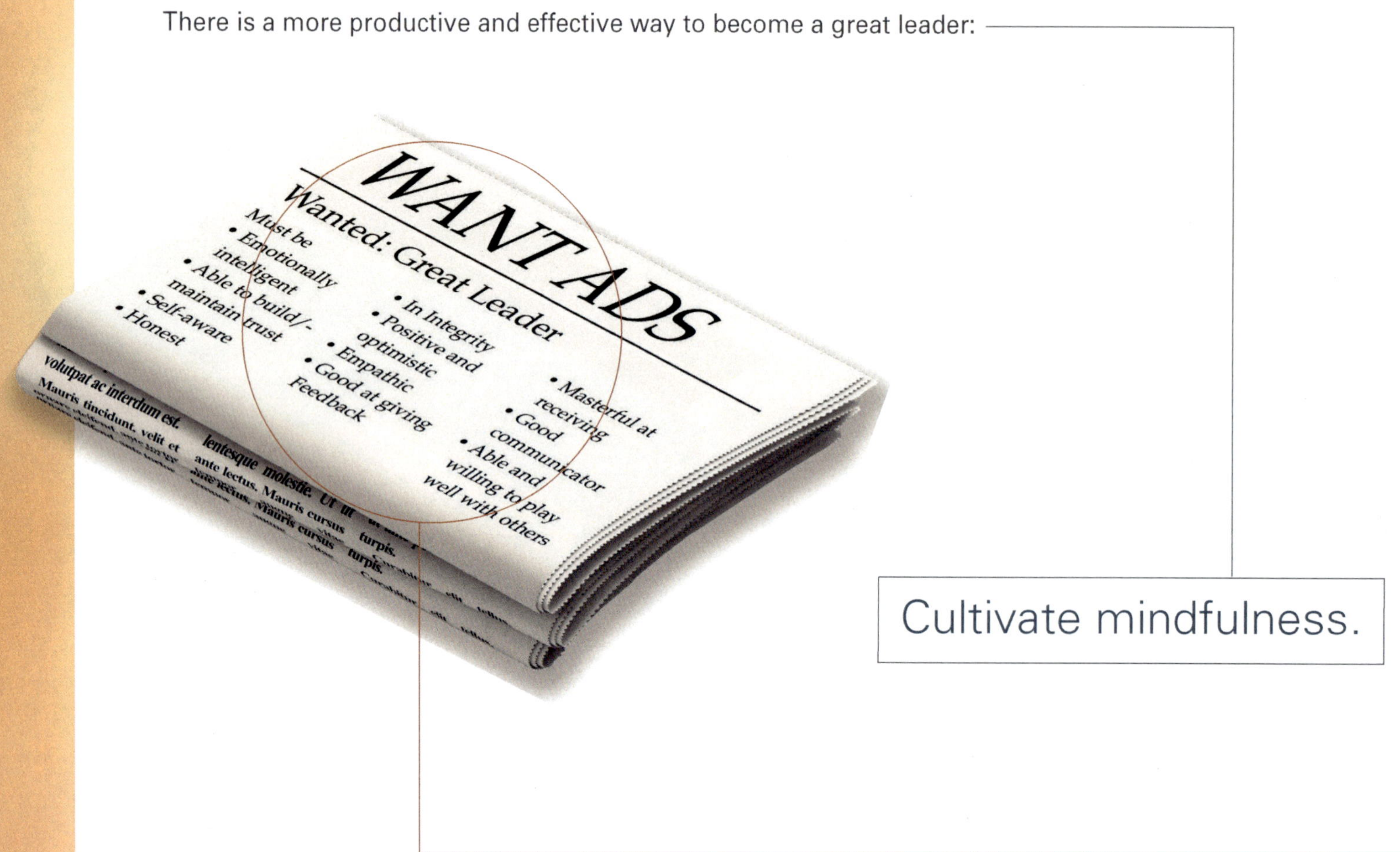

Cultivate mindfulness.

Put another way, when a person has cultivated mindful awareness, leadership itself becomes a way of being, a natural response to what is happening in the surrounding environment. It becomes less of a strategy or list of qualities to be mastered.

Cultivating mindfulness works at the source (the "Self") to develop naturally brilliant leaders.

If you are to successfully lead an organization today, then mindfulness is no longer optional. Mindfulness is critical for leading well. In fact, once you've adopted the mindful approach, you'll find it's critical for *living* well.

Mindfulness = better leadership

I would be turning my back on everything I believe in if I were to promote mindfulness primarily as a shortcut to professional development.

If you undertake mindfulness practices to "get" something, you are certain to be disappointed, as striving to acquire things runs counter to the practice of developing mindful awareness.

Gaining and improving mindful awareness is a journey you will travel for the rest of your life. So, rather than thinking of this program as a shortcut to another goal, I encourage you to see it as an alternative path that improves with practice. Mindfulness is both the journey and the destination.

WANT ADS
Wanted: Great Leader
Must be
• Mindful

Understanding Mindfulness

What exactly is mindfulness, and how does one cultivate it?

Mindfulness is the *moment-to-moment awareness and acceptance of what's going on within us and in the world around us.* To be mindful gives you the ability to choose, at any moment, to witness or observe your own thoughts and feelings (physical and emotional), acknowledge them, and let them go. That part of you that does the witnessing or observing is what we refer to as the Self.

Sounds simple, right? It is, and it's not.

To be mindful is to pay attention to what is right here, right now, in the present moment—never the past, never the future. Mindfulness is observing all your thoughts, emotions, and physical feelings without judgment.

I heard a wise person define the human being as "biology with a voiceover." When we are mindless, our minds are filled with a random cacophony of thoughts . *Mindlessness* is a state of distraction that focuses on nothing of importance—daydreaming, in essence—when something in front of us requires our attention. Being mindless is being "spaced out."

In contrast, when the mind is clear and settled we are free to be present. Athletes and artists often refer to this mindful state as "in the zone," a state of being from which they perform or create at their peak. Nothing seemingly exists but the game, the ball, the instrument, the audience. Everything flows.

With practice, we can break free of mindlessness, and enter the zone of mindfulness.

Let's take a walk through the difference between mindlessness and mindfulness.

A mindless experience

Imagine that you see a new red convertible go by and think to yourself, *"There goes a new red convertible,"* followed in the next millisecond by, *"Man that's such a sweet car,"*... *"I want a car like that,"*... *"Steve drove a car like that and he's a jerk,"*... *"That guy's probably a jerk too,"*... *"Look who's having a midlife crisis,"*... *"What model of Ferrari is that?"*... and on and on and on...

In this scenario, a car became the trigger for a flood of stories jumping around inside the mind.

A mindful experience

Imagine you see that new red convertible go by and think, *"There goes a new red convertible... and now here comes the next car."*

Alternately, when you see the new red convertible go by and catch yourself meandering down the, "I want a car like that and Steve is a jerk" road, you pause and observe those thoughts, witnessing them as they move across the screen of your mind. You recognize them as simply being thoughts and made-up stories you don't need to do anything about. You may even become curious or amused that Steve still triggers you.

In mindfulness, there are variations on two thoughts: "Look at what's happening here," and "Hmmm, that's interesting." The very next thought that comments further comes from ego, from the brain. And that's not bad—it can even be useful or insightful. It's just not mindful. (Comically, my own ego chatter during meditation often has to do with how to write or teach about mindfulness!)

Through meditation, this kind of mindful awareness becomes our default setting. Meditating is practicing mindfulness in an intentional and structured way. With regular practice, the brain becomes skilled at settling down and quietly observing, and a peaceful mind becomes the "new normal."

Within the next few weeks of regular practice you will experience the new normal for yourself.

70% of executives report that they regularly daydream during meetings.[2]

So, mindfulness is paying attention to what you are doing, feeling, and thinking at the time you are actually doing, feeling, and thinking it.

Sounds simple enough, doesn't it?

Yet, if you have ever tried to focus your attention for any length of time, you know just how challenging it can be.

Many of us notice, as we begin to cultivate mindfulness, just how distracted or preoccupied we are much of the time, and such a state of being impedes our quality of life and undermines our leadership.

When we live *without* moment-to-moment awareness we:

- *Drive home on "auto-pilot" and can't recall the trip*
- *Daydream*
- *Check our phone, even though we just checked it*
- *Graze the refrigerator when bored*
- *Race to to reach our destinations faster*
- *Forget a person's name almost as soon as they are introduced to us*
- *Get so focused on a goal that we let other important things slide*

This is no trivial matter. The average American spends 18 hours of their workweek spacing out! A comprehensive study undertaken by Harvard University found that, on average, we are ***not present*** for 47% of our waking lives. We are most likely to drift off when we are at the office and when someone else is talking to us.[3]

Our minds need occasional breaks, right?

Daydreaming may seem restful—our minds need occasional breaks, right?

Neuroscience research reveals that exactly the opposite is true. Wandering minds cause us to be less happy and less satisfied.[4] Here's the irony: even if our minds wander off to ***positive*** memories (past) or ***positive*** anticipation (future) it still causes an overall decrease in happiness.[5]

Occasionally, we can replay the parts of our life that we missed. We can read the page a second time or ask the person we just met to repeat their name. However, most of our mindless moments go unnoticed and unclaimed—minutes, hours, and eventually years

Lost.

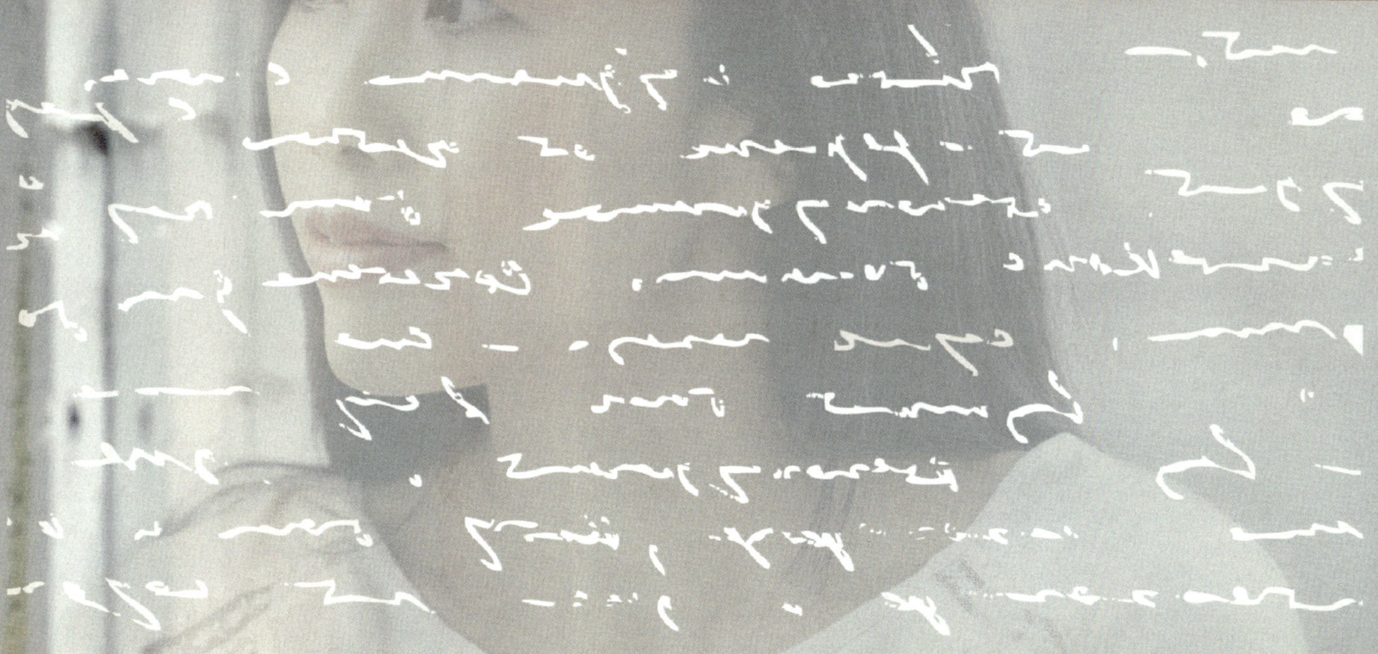

Bottom line: You may be missing out on half of your life, and your organization may only have half a leader.

When we don't accept what's going on within us and in the world around us,

We find ourselves in bad moods for no apparent reason

We hold tension in our necks, backs, or shoulders

We try always to look on the "bright side"

We feel stressed out or burned out

We find escape in TV, alcohol, and other drugs

We repeatedly recall our worst fears

We try to talk ourselves out of uncomfortable thoughts and feelings

We become easily frustrated by people and circumstances

Although we may use some of these strategies as coping skills, they are actually tell-tale signs of mindlessness. When we are unable or unwilling to accept things exactly the way they are then we get stuck. We may rail against reality by insisting, "It's not supposed to be like this!" But guess what—it *is* like this. When we resist what is in the present then our snow globe becomes agitated and cloudy.

E

F P

T O Z

L P E D

P E C F D

E D F C Z P

F E L O P Z D

seeing clearly is impossible.

D E F P O T E

L K O I W E U G S

When an individual lives mindlessly, their work suffers.

Mindfulness and Mono-tasking

Often worn as a badge of honor, multitasking is driven by the need to accomplish more in less time. Yet, multitasking seldom produces a quality outcome. Research has demonstrated that we may *feel* more productive but that productivity actually drops when we attempt to do several things simultaneously. As a result, we are less satisfied with our lives. If you sit at your desk while eating lunch and checking your email then neither task will receive your full attention and you have little chance of fully enjoying your meal.

Beyond multitasking, we find what researcher Linda Stone calls ***Continuous Partial Attention***. Stone argues that when leaders give only partial attention to every moment, the underlying driver is not the simple desire to do more in less time. Rather, Continuous Partial Attention grows out of a compulsive need to connect and be connected as we hurtle through our lives.

Stone's research shows that many of us scatter our attention by constantly scanning life in an attempt to "optimize for the best opportunities, activities, and contacts, in any given moment. We compulsively stay at the center of whatever is going on." Stone writes, "To be busy, to be connected, is to be alive, to be recognized, and to matter."

Many, if not most, of the executives who enter our programs are stuck in Continuous Partial Attention. Their eyes dart about the room as they text away, holding their cell phones on their laps below the conference table, hoping no one will notice—planning meetings, issuing directives, their minds anything but settled. The cost of this scattered energy is high indeed.

Our drive to remain at the center of it all causes us to become overwhelmed, overstimulated, overworked, and overloaded.

Something must give.

When a leader lives mindlessly, their entire organization suffers.

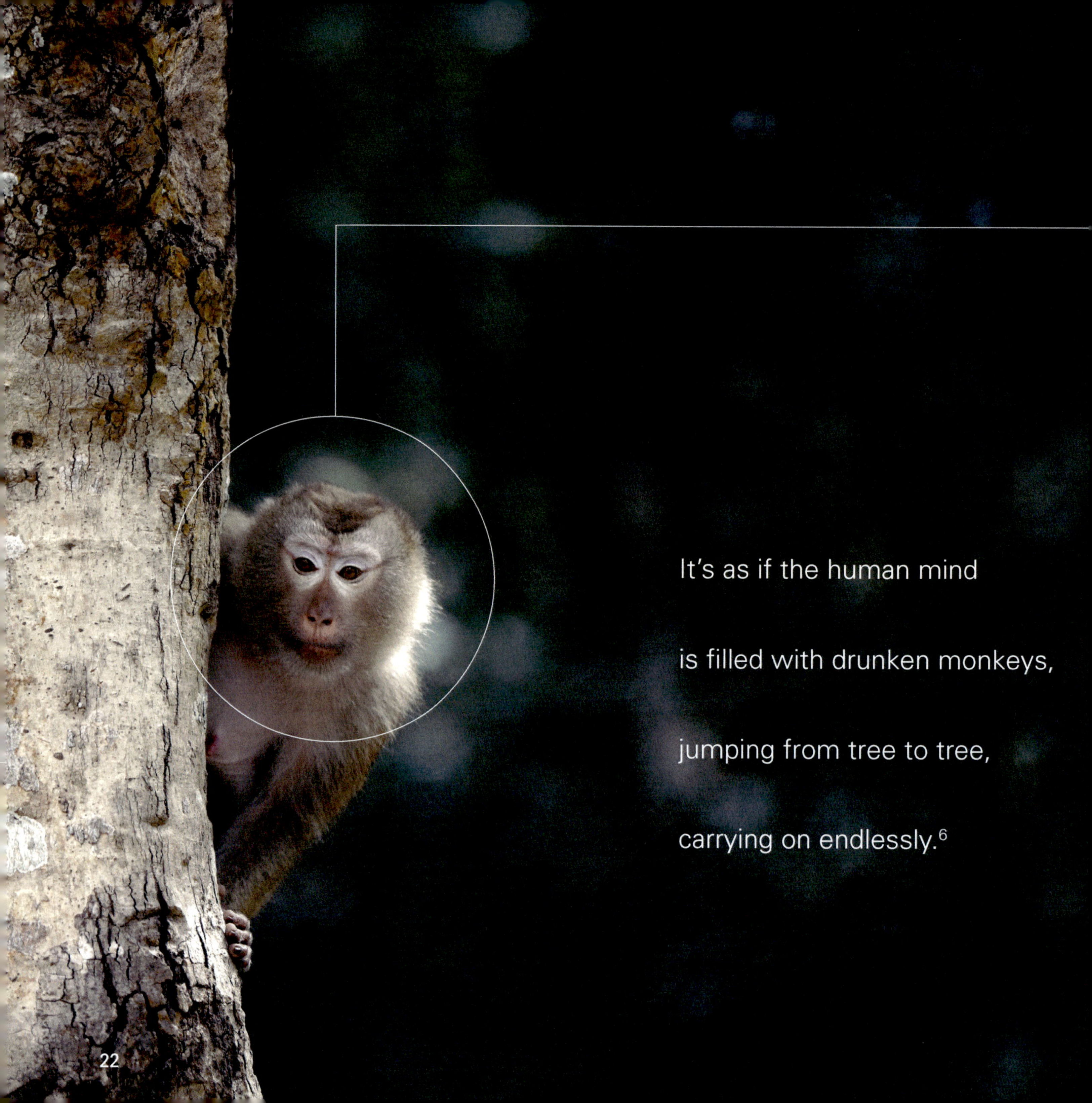

It's as if the human mind

is filled with drunken monkeys,

jumping from tree to tree,

carrying on endlessly.[6]

Mindfulness and Leadership

Through mindful awareness, we learn to focus our attention on one thing at a time. We complete each thought before taking up the next. We remain focused and clear-headed. We effectively optimize ourselves.

Following are some ways mindfulness can optimize your efforts and improve your leadership. Yet, mindfulness is more than a means to an end or a tool for professional success. I include these, in hope that the tangible benefits of mindfulness will inspire you to undertake your own daily practice, through which you will discover that the most transformational benefits go far beyond leadership skills. Mindfulness is a door through which you can step into a finer, happier, more fulfilling life.

Productivity

Strange but true, ***we can increase our productivity by learning to do nothing.*** But mindfulness is not an empty nothing. Mindfulness teachers call the practice of doing nothing ***"non-doing,"*** which involves learning to cease activity and to just be, taking it all in. Paradoxically, by becoming skilled at non-doing, once you return to doing, the quality of your work and your life will have improved.[7]

True masters of any discipline make their work look easy. Masters of mindfulness are never in a frenzy; they always have or make time to give you their undivided attention.

Emotional Intelligence

Here's a crazy statistic: people get hired largely for their hard skills, such as education, credentials, and experience. But once hired, ***job success and upward mobility depend 85 percent*** on soft skills, like self-awareness and emotional intelligence, and only 15 percent on the hard skills it took to land the job.[8]

What exactly is emotional intelligence (other than a faddish business buzzword)? Emotional Intelligence (EQ) is the "ability to recognize, understand and manage our own emotions, combined with the ability to recognize, understand and influence the emotions of others."[9] EQ is the single best predictor of job and leadership success and failure. The primary causes of executive derailment involve deficiencies in emotional competence.[10]

Overwhelming data shows that EQ is a critical factor in leadership success. Here's one example: Rutgers University conducted a study in which supervisors received training in emotional intelligence. The results: lost time incidents decreased by 50 percent and grievances decreased from 15 per year to just 3. The plant went on to exceed its productivity goals by $250,000.[11]

Cultivating EQ significantly overlaps with cultivating mindfulness but with one important distinction. In mindfulness, we stop short of trying to "influence the emotions of others." However, a mindful person's influence is more powerful because there is never a secret agenda.

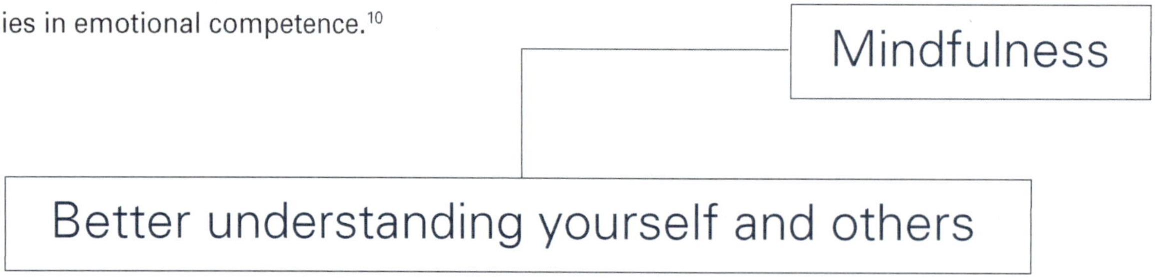

Mindfulness

Better understanding yourself and others

Unless I can bring myself into that stressful environment in a steady and mindful way, be present in the moment, at every opportunity, I can't help the people around me and lead them.

Mark T. Bertolini, CEO, Aetna

Employee Engagement and Turnover

Let's get something straight. People don't quit their jobs. They quit their bosses. 75 percent of working adults report that the most stressful aspect of their job is their immediate boss.[12] The inability of many leaders to create and maintain a positive working relationship may explain why nearly 50 percent of U.S. adults surveyed have left a job, "to get away from their manager."[13]

While not enough studies have been completed to determine whether mindfulness can make a boss more "likeable," thereby improving employee retention, there is mounting evidence to suggest that it can. It makes sense: When your state of mind is unsettled or when you are preoccupied, being in tune with your direct reports or the broader team is likely to go out the window. Your stress becomes their stress. If you take out your stress on them, or if you are unable to function as a buffer for them, their morale will suffer.

Mindfulness

Retained employee

Mindfulness
Stress reduction

Stress Reduction

If you are a leader, you are undoubtedly under enormous pressure most of the time. The stress of leading an organization is staggering and ever-increasing. Since we cannot slow the rate of change, we must find effective ways to maintain balance and thrive while life whizzes by at warp speed, while market conditions evolve rapidly.

Jon Kabat-Zinn, Professor of Medicine Emeritus, University of Massachusetts Medical School, is a pioneer in Mindfulness-Based Stress Reduction (MBSR). For three decades Kabat-Zinn has offered eight-week mindfulness courses and studied their effects. MBSR, which is now offered at medical centers around the world, has proved that undertaking a regular practice of awareness exercises significantly lessens anxiety, depression, and chronic fatigue—and that eight weeks is long enough to see significant improvement.[14]

Interestingly, it's not clear how much of this stress reduction is "cause" and how much is "effect." Along with decreased stress, participants also report improved relationships with family and coworkers. As people interact with the world more thoughtfully and skillfully, they tend to provoke those around them less often, which in turn, reduces the likelihood that stress-filled situations will arise.

Undertaking a regular practice of awareness exercises has added benefits, including reversing some of the effects of aging on the brain,[15] improving memory,[16] increasing immune function,[17] and decreasing pain.[18]

Jeff Bezos
CEO, Amazon

It takes courage to say 'Wait. Slow down. Get more information.' Perhaps even (gasp) ask for help. Begin to unhook from cultural expectations of how to do it (whatever it is), and instead, cultivate the elegant discipline of getting at the deeper truths. Take your business, and your life, into your own hands with a mindfulness practice.

Oprah Winfrey

(On stillness) ...where all creative expression, peace, light and love come to be. Only from that space can you create your best work, and your best life.

speak on Mindfulness

Bill Ford

CEO, Ford Motor Company

The practice of mindfulness kept me going during the darkest days.

Jeff Weiner

CEO, LinkedIn

Developing a mindfulness practice will benefit you more than any other single thing you can do in your life. If you wish to transform yourself, company and world, then developing a mindfulness practice is a must.

Cultivating Mindfulness

Good news!
You already know how to become mindful.

1. ***Stop for a moment*** *right now and take a... long... deep... luxurious breath.*

2. ***Now, slowly take one more****, and this time notice how good your lungs feel when they are full, and how your body relaxes as you deflate completely.*

That's pretty much it.

Our intention is to take that single and simple experience of being 100 percent conscious and support you in creating more and more room for these moments of mindfulness. Gradually, as your mind settles, you will be able to stay present for longer periods and you will begin to notice a cascade of positive effects.

During this program, you will be invited to try a variety of techniques designed to help settle the mind. They include both formal practices (sitting meditation and journaling) and informal micro-practices (eating mindfully and silently offering loving kindness to each person you encounter).

Some of these practices you will find suit you more than others. But there is no substitute for the basic mindfulness practice of breathing deeply and becoming aware of what's going on inside you and around you. Lifelong masters of mindfulness make adjustments to their practice as their own needs change. But those who cut back on the time and energy they devote to their practice always note a change that has them wanting to spend more time, rather than less time, in the "present moment."

As a participant in this program, you will develop:

- *a quieter and more settled mind*
- *ability to focus your attention*
- *awareness of the ego*
- *decreased stress and anxiety*
- *greater self confidence*
- *real-time access to wisdom*
- *ability to relax and to play*
- *faster recovery after setbacks*

Yes This program can generate measurable positive effects in your leadership and in your life. Leaders studied before and after practicing mindfulness for eight weeks showed improved function of their brains, stress levels, and overall health.[19] Surprisingly, the benefits may appear much sooner than eight weeks. As little as five days of brief meditation has been found to improve stress regulation and to decrease the incidence of anxiety, depression, and anger.[20]

Is it really possible to

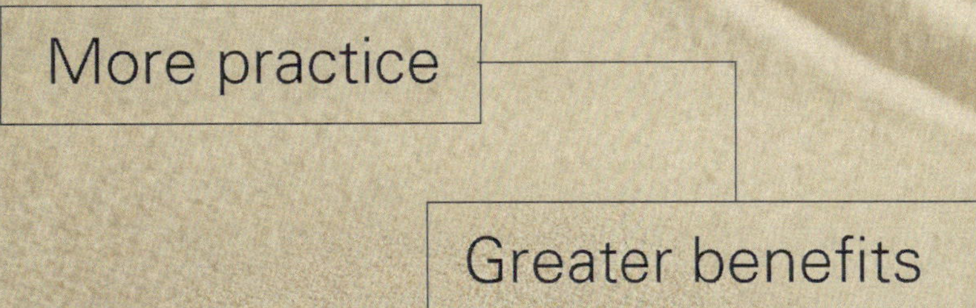

do all that in 8 weeks?

and: No The benefits of cultivating mindfulness are dose-dependent. The more you practice, the greater the benefits. If you follow this program then eight weeks is plenty of time to develop the habit of mindfulness and to see real improvements in your life. Yet the work itself will take the rest of your life, sometimes with big improvements, sometimes with incremental or even hard-to-notice improvements. (But that's OK. You learn not to be attached to improving).

Over the coming eight weeks you will be training your brain, like one would train for an athletic competition. Brain training requires daily practice even on the days you don't feel like it. An athlete can't expect to see results if they wake each morning and consider in that moment, whether or not they feel like training that day. The same goes for training yourself to become more mindful. If you are spotty in your daily practice then you will probably be disappointed by the outcome, feel like it's not working, and quit.

Habit energy is stronger than volition. Thich Nhat Hahn

Anyone who has ever invested time and energy toward reaching a worthy goal knows the wisdom of Brene Brown's words, "The willingness to show up changes us. It makes us a little braver each time." This is absolutely true when it comes to mindfulness, and specifically, meditation. If you can get yourself into the chair each day then the rest is easy.

Commitment = progress

The Program

If you have time to breathe,

you have time to meditate.

You breathe when you walk.

You breathe when you stand.

You breathe when you lie down.

Ajahn Amaro

Formal Practice

Throughout the coming eight weeks, each day you will be invited to practice mindful awareness both formally and informally.

Formal practice includes multiple forms of meditation and journaling. Guided meditations for each day are available on the free app that accompanies this book. The first week's meditation is seven minutes long with much "guiding." By the end of the program, you will be sitting for 15 minutes each day, mostly in silence.

Informal Practice

Informal practices are ways of incorporating mindful awareness during the remaining 23 hours and 45 minutes of the day. This is because no amount of meditation will be enough to redeem the rest of the day if it is spent mindlessly. Patiently, through informal practice, you will learn to bring mindful awareness to every activity from leading a board meeting to washing dishes.

> *We don't have to schedule a trip to the monastery to enjoy the benefits of mindfulness. We can use many 'ordinary' events in our daily lives to call us back to ourselves and to the present moment.* Thich Nhat Hahn

Failing at Mindfulness

You will not be perfect in your practice—maybe not even close. Likely, and despite your best intentions, there will be times you just don't get to it. Go easy on yourself. Remember, mindfulness is "moment-to-moment awareness *with acceptance.*" Simply accept that you've not done what you committed to do, and then notice if you're judging yourself. The truth is, even if you are a Tibetan monk, your practice could always improve. That's why we practice kindness and gentleness with ourselves first.

If your practice goes off the rails completely, accept it. Do not allow your brain to berate you. Simply pick yourself up and begin again. Mindfulness is a cross-country run, not a sprint.

Getting Ready – Pulling Back the Bow

Imagine you are an archer. You raise the bow, hold it firmly with one hand. With the other, you pull back the string, aiming carefully. The stronger you pull back the farther and faster your arrow will fly. The more carefully you aim, the better the chance you have of hitting your target.

With your mindfulness practice in sight, now is the time to pull back and prepare. Before beginning your mindfulness practice, consider your target. Without a steady target you've nothing to aim for. Set an intention for yourself (we'll get to this). Consider what it is that you have to pull back in order to strengthen the flight of your arrow—the path to your goal.

Then let go...

You are on your way!

Set the start date

Rather than just sliding into the program with the turn of a page, give yourself the best possible chance of successfully practicing daily. Consider beginning on a weekend before you have to balance your new practice with weekday obligations.

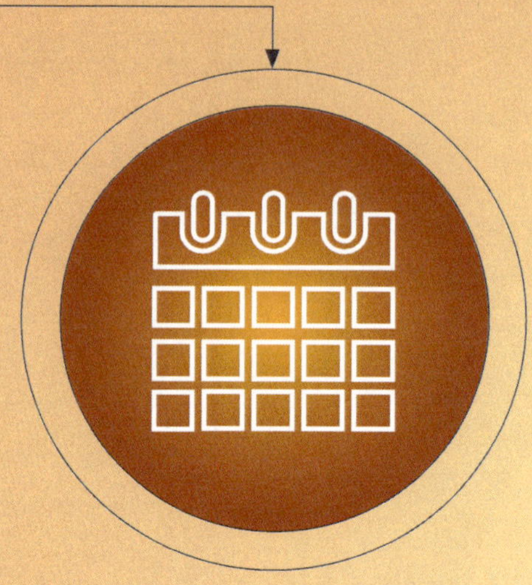

Set the time

Initially, set aside seven minutes each day. While any time of the day will do, most people who practice consistently prefer the morning, before the busyness of a normal day intrudes or exhaustion turns the exercise into an impromptu nap.

Tip: *Practicing at the same time each day can help establish a healthy habit.*

Ready your quiet space

Find a comfortable, reasonably quiet place where you can just "be" without much interruption. As with choosing the same time each day, the same place each day is helpful in creating habits that stick. Most any spot with a bench, chair, or even a seating cushion will do.

It's fine if there is some background noise but preferably not wildly distracting.

Tip: *If your home is too full of activity in the morning, try driving to work 15 minutes early. After arriving, do the exercise while you are still parked in the car. Consider it your four-wheeled cone-of-silence. For extra effectiveness, try sitting in the back seat or even the passenger seat, where your mental associations of being behind the wheel will be minimized.*

Determine your "WHY"

Considering why you are undertaking a mindfulness program will support your process and help keep you on track. See the following page for your first journaling exercise.

Get the app

Download the free app that accompanies this program which contains a guided meditation for each week. The app offers optional reminders—as many as three times a day—to bring you back to awareness when the speed of your day picks up.

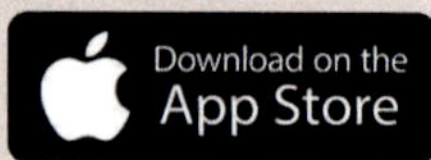

Start your journal

Throughout this program you will be invited to journal. We have set aside pages within the book for you to write on. Alternatively, you may decide you prefer to use your own journal to mark the beginning of this program.

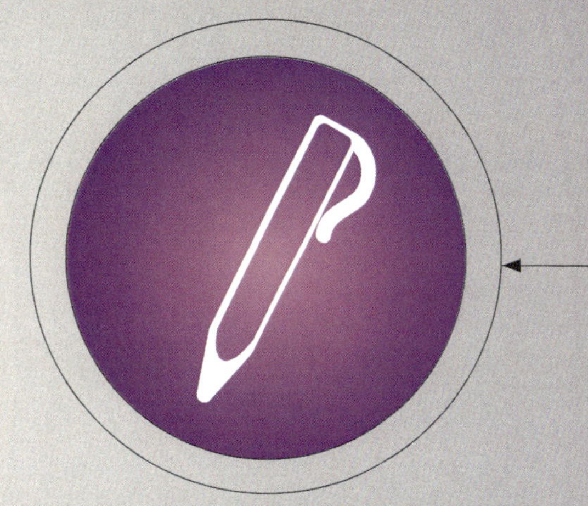

Are you ready?

 *Start date set*

 *Time set*

 *Quiet spot readied*

 *App downloaded*

 *Journal and pen (This book or bound journal)*

Journal

Finding Your "Why"

You are not here by accident. Something about this work has piqued your interest. What was it that drew you to this program? Why now?

Imagine

yourself with a quieter, more settled mind, living with moment to moment awareness and acceptance. How might your life be different from how it is today?

Who, besides you,

stands to benefit as you increase your mindful awareness?

Summarizing

your journaling, why do you want to become more mindful?

Stop and write yourself an invitation

On your start date, bring this book and your smartphone (the app downloaded) to the quiet place you've set aside for meditating.

I'll meet you there.

Dear Self,
You are cordially
invited to join me for
this special event.
Start Date:
Time:
Place:

Week 1

Noticing your Attention

Imagine your attention is a spotlight that comes right out from between your eyes, like a miner's head lamp. As your spotlight moves, your attention follows, focusing on whatever the light is shining on.

Often our spotlights move around all on their own, wherever they feel like taking us. You may be in a meeting, listening to someone speak, and your spotlight wanders to what you will cook for dinner or if you're going to get that promotion.

You wanted to listen, but your spotlight moved off in other directions.

Sometimes you may follow your spotlight into the past: rehashing, reminiscing, remembering, ruminating. At other times, you may follow it into the future: planning, rehearsing, fantasizing, or worrying.

We look to our leaders to show us a compelling vision of the future and how we can get there together. When a leader becomes distracted by each new interest and concern, it creates organizational whiplash, which ultimately undermines trust and confidence in the leadership.

Our first step towards mindfulness is simply to notice where our attention is going.

This week

Notice where your Spotlight of Awareness is pointing from moment to moment. When you are sitting in meditation and when you are going about your day, observe the path of your attention and where your focus lands (this is an important informal micropractice). Does your spotlight return to the same places often? Do you daydream? Do you rehash or rehearse? Once you begin your practice of noticing, you may discover that your attention is being dragged all over the place. Don't judge it, push it, or pull it. Just notice. Later in the program we'll work on where you'll want your attention to go.

This week, when you realize that your attention has wandered,

Celebrate!

That is a moment
of mindful awareness.

The Basics of Meditation

This first week, our meditation focuses on sitting and breathing. That may sound odd given that you have been sitting and breathing successfully for some time now.

However, mindful sitting and breathing has a different quality to it. As we sit and breathe in meditation, that is *all* we are doing. This is a form of *non-doing*, which paradoxically, may be hard to *do*. Ironically, dedication and effort are required if you want to master *non-doing*.

Meditation trains the brain to focus on one thing at a time.

Although your intent may be to sit and do nothing, your mind may not be a willing partner. As soon as you begin to meditate, your monkey mind will jump about screeching and screaming, trying desperately to get your attention, insisting that you get up and do something! Anything!

This is to be expected.

Welcome to meditation!

Meditating

Each morning I sit on the floor in the middle of our guest room.

I take a few deep breaths and allow my eyes to close.

I focus on the feeling of my breath, as my stomach expands and contracts. In… and out… in… and out… in and ... it's Thursday. That's trash day. Before I leave for the office I need to wheel the trash to the curb... ooops, I'm off-task. Back to my breath. In… and out… in… and what if I forget to take the trash out? How will I remember? Maybe I better stop and write myself a note, then get back to meditating. No, that's just a thought. Back to the breath… in… and out… in and...

Meditation is not stopping thoughts or achieving a blank mind. Meditation is the practice of thinking only one thought at a time.

Some meditators imagine their thoughts like clouds floating by, without needing to stop or hang onto them—just watching as they float on by.

Another way of looking at it is like riding a bike: We maintain balance by continuously making micro-corrections. When we veer slightly to the right, we instinctively lean left to restore balance. Meditation is similar. As you sit, your mind will veer off slightly, and it's your job to restore balance by making those slight corrections. Yes, sometimes you'll tip over completely. That's the time to pick yourself up, dust off, and get back on the bike.

Breathing effectively

The basic technique used by most people is simple: Breathe in through your nose and out through your mouth. That's all. As for the depth of the breath, breathe into your belly. Notice if your chest tends to fill up first; if it does, work on bringing your breath down to the belly instead. For extra credit, breathe deeply enough to expand the upper ribs of your back before exhaling. If you have gotten used to the in/nose, out/mouth breath, you can experiment with in/nose, out/nose when extra calm is needed.

I once heard that one of the reasons cigarette smoking is so comforting is because smokers are accustomed to taking deep breaths to inhale and exhale properly. You will find the simple act of breathing deeply, in through your nose, and out through your mouth, is deeply calming and much better for you.

Position and posture for meditation

You can meditate in any position you wish as long as you can remain relaxed and alert. But note that for most people, lying down, while relaxing, causes sleep—not the best outcome!

If this is your first time meditating, we suggest you sit in a chair with both feet flat on the floor—legs not crossed—and your hands resting in your lap or on your thighs.

It is preferable (but not necessary) to sit up tall, instead of leaning back on the chair, because it is easier to remain alert when you are erect.

That's it.

Of course, you can take a more traditional approach if you wish, seated on the floor with a meditation bench, pad, or pillow. For our purposes, any posture that allows you to remain relaxed and alert, sitting up straight (or at least not slouched) is perfect.

Keeping it simple limits obstacles to getting started.

Here we go!

Please get comfortable in your quiet spot, and listen to the Introduction and Week 1 Meditation.

Journal Week One

In the first few days *of this program, I was surprised by...*

When I think about *taking time for "non-doing," it makes me feel...*

Where would my *leadership benefit from some "non-doing?"*

My Spotlight of Awareness *often...*

I enjoyed a moment *of mindfulness when...*

Week 2

Quieting the Chatter

Imagine that you have a roommate and the one thing your roommate loves to do is TALK. No matter where you are or what you are doing... your roommate is right there too, jabbering away, following you from room to room, trying to engage you in conversation while you are on the computer, or cleaning the kitchen, or trying to watch the ball game. Even as you drift off to sleep at night your roommate is right there, sitting on the side of your bed, saying "blah, blah, blah, blah."

The crazy part is

... that you don't have to imagine it at all. You've got one. If you are like every other human being, you have a voice inside your head that narrates your life, whether you want it or not. Most of us live unaware that we have an inner roommate. We have grown so accustomed to the incessant chatter and narration that we actually identify with it as who we are.

You might be wondering right about now, "What the heck does this have to do with leadership?" Good question! The answer is... everything! YOU have amazing potential as a leader. Unfortunately, your roommate doesn't.

Yet you listen to your roommate and seldom question his or her judgment. In fact, your roommate has landed a job as your personal motivational coach, and your coach's words inspire your emotions. If your coach tells you you're a failure, you believe what he or she says, and your heart tells you you're a failure too. Your coach tells you that your boss is unfair, and pretty soon feelings of resentment arise to match the coaching. Next thing you know, you're actually thanking your roommate-coach for enlightening you, for telling you the truth.

Truth be told, your roommate is a crappy leader, so getting a handle on this predicament will make an immediate and incredible impact.

If you don't, then the next time you need to give someone constructive feedback, you might find your roommate doing all the talking. You may find your roommate jumping in to help manage your time, resolve conflicts, and plan your future. These are tasks your roommate is terrible at!

Some inner roommates are kind and supportive. Mine is not. Mine is a critic. Maybe yours is too. My roommate reminds me over and over about where I have fallen short, what other people do better than I do, and why I should not venture into new territory (like writing this book). Once I began to pay attention, I found that my inner roommate speaks to me in ways I would never allow another human being to speak to me. How is your inner roommate treating you?

You may begin to notice how unfriendly some of that chatter is, delivering a litany of discouragements and predictions of doom that may sound like any of these:

"You're not good/smart/beautiful/young enough."

"Why did you say that? You sounded like such an idiot!"

"You're in over your head this time."

"You really blew it."

"You're a failure."

"What if the worst happens?"

"Good things don't last, at least not for you."

"Ignore that feeling. That's too much—stuff it."

Sound familiar? Here's the thing: none of them are true. Not one of them. Each one of these, and their many variants, is mindlessness at its greatest force. We're not born with these thoughts; we inherit them from our family, our society, the media. None of us are immune.

What do you replace these nasty statements with? You might consider replacing them with a self-affirming statement like, "I love myself," or better yet, you might consider replacing them with... nothing.

The beauty of mindfulness is the feeling of spaciousness that replaces the drone of the roommate—not the emptiness of loneliness or purposelessness, but rather the emptiness of space, of stillness, of neither "good" nor "bad," just presence—a full experience of the present moment.

The next time you notice your roommate battering away at you, tune it out. That voice is not the real you.

This week

Remember, your mind is your domain!
You have a right to live in peace.

Bad news: There's no use trying to evict your roommate, as they are not going anywhere.

Good news: Through awareness and self-observation, you can break free of your roommate's control. This week, we will practice taking the ***Seat of the Witness.*** During the meditation and throughout your day, notice what your roommate is saying—the way you noticed your Spotlight of Awareness last week.

Don't try to stop your inner roommate from talking, and definitely don't argue with them—they always win! Notice what your roommate has to say and how it makes you feel. Simply witness the litany of thoughts as they pass through your mind, without becoming entangled in them. Let any feelings that arise as reactions to your roommate's chatter drift away.

For particularly insistent thoughts, remind yourself, "That's just my roommate. I don't need to do anything about that."

This week we are simply becoming aware of what our minds have been up to all along. We will also introduce a body scan, which will be explored more deeply in later weeks.

Journal Week Two

My inner roommate *gets really loud when...*

At work *my inner roommate is relentless when it comes to...*

I allow my inner roommate *to influence my feelings about...*

I'm more able *to take the Seat of the Witness when...*

Week 3

The mind is its own place, and in itself can make a heaven of hell, a hell of heaven...

Michael Singer, The Untethered Soul

Outsmarting your Brain

By now you will have noticed that remaining mindful (in or out of meditation) may not be easy. This is, in part, due to inherited traits. In fact, we are genetically predisposed *not* to be mindful. Instead, we are wired to:

- *continuously scan for danger and threats*
- *get into thinking ruts*
- *react impulsively*

These tendencies are hard-wired within us from birth. To live mindfully, we need to overcome our biology, physiology, and chemistry. We need to rewire our brains.

Why should we develop in ways that go against our very nature? After all, as the old television commercial bellowed, "It's not nice to fool Mother Nature!"

Evolutionarily speaking, we are only wired to be successful. Professor Ronald D. Siegel of Harvard Medical School reminds us, "We were made to be successful hominids, not happy hominids." Happiness, fulfillment, and wisdom do not arise from survival instincts. As a leader, you will find many of your instincts will not serve you well at all.

Let's explore these genetic propensities one at a time, understanding how the old wiring functions, and how new wiring can better support your leadership.

Scanning for Threats

Remember the Spotlight of Awareness? It has one supremely important function: to stand like a watchman, vigilantly scanning the horizon for potential threats and dangers. This thought-habit kept our ancestors safe back in the days when they dwelt among the elements and predators.

Today, we rarely face life-threatening danger, although our spotlight continues to scan for threats in our boss's words, the business section of the newspaper or the new org chart. All of these needlessly activate our fight or flight instincts and cause our bodies and minds to experience the same reactions our ancestors had when encountering true dangers. Our *bodies* don't know the difference.

We evolved perfectly to react to possible danger and then to return to a normal state once the threat had passed. The trouble is that many of us never actually return to a true normal state. Those day-to-day stressors cause us to remain in a constant state of high alert, which over time, degrades nearly every system in the body (from digestive, to heart, to sexual function).[21] Getting stuck in high alert causes us to become stressed out, sick, and ineffective.

> *I have lived through a lot of terrible things in my life. Some of them actually happened.*
> Mark Twain

The instinct to scan for threats and dangers, which has kept us safe for millennia, has become maladaptive and often hinders our ability to lead well and decreases our overall quality of life.[22]

Thinking Ruts

Once thought to be fixed in our early twenties, our brains are now known to change and adapt throughout our lives. Through the process of neuroplasticity, our brains "beef up" the neural pathways that are used the most.

For instance, before GPS, London cabbies were required to memorize 25,000 streets and thousands of landmarks before they were given their license, sometimes requiring years to learn. When a group of experienced cabbies was studied (relative to non-cabbies), the portion of the brain used for spatial mapping had grown more robust. The repeated work of memorizing maps had increased those neural connections.[23]

Think of it like a highway

When there is a lot of traffic on a particular neural pathway, the brain can widen that highway, readying it for even ***more*** traffic.

Neuroplasticity causes our brains to widen the highway for anything we do extensively over long periods of time. Here's the catch: when we experience worry, fear, stress, and anger, our brains adapt to that too, readying the highway for even ***more*** of the same traffic. Eventually we need to experience that negative emotion just to feel normal.

Through mindfulness practices we can dissolve these thinking ruts and intentionally "beef up" the portions of our brains that make us happier, healthier, wiser, and more creative, while allowing the less useful pathways to recede.

Though significantly rewiring the brain requires dedicated practice over a long period of time, even a little bit of meditation can support new, more positive habits in our thinking.[24]

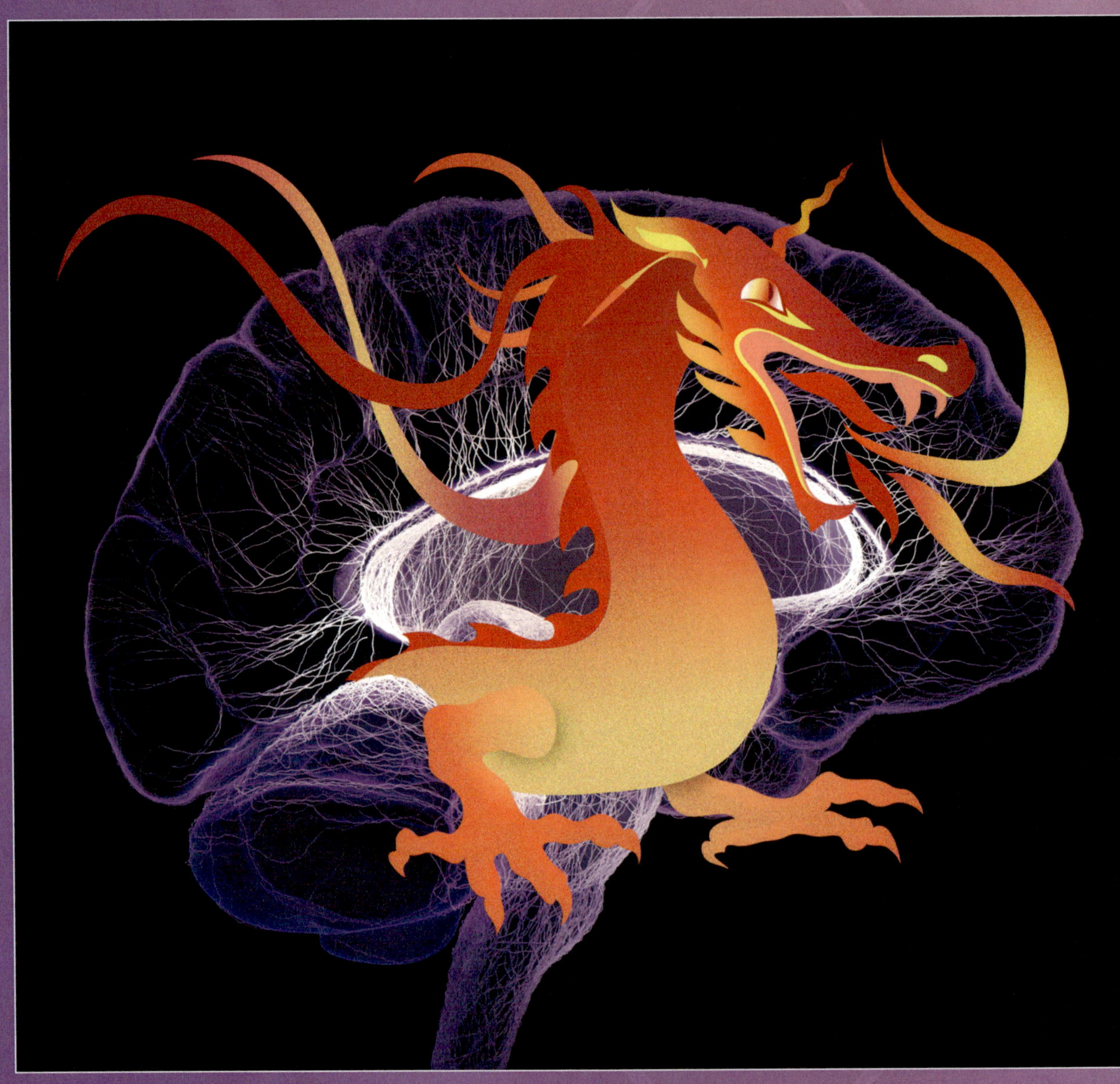

Reacting Impulsively

When your brain registers a stimulus, it travels a known pathway beginning at the amygdala, a small almond-shaped structure at the base of your brain. Evolutionarily speaking, the amygdala is the oldest region of the brain and is sometimes referred to as the Reptilian Brain or the Lizard Brain. Tasked with asking and answering the question, "Is this imminently dangerous?" the Lizard Brain is there to protect us. When it senses immediate danger, it kicks in and instantly propels us to fight, flee, or freeze.

Occasionally our Lizard Brains are useful. But these days they get us *into* more trouble than they get us *out of* by continually firing, even when there are no actual threats to our *physical* safety. They can be triggered by a mean-spirited email, a moment of public embarrassment, or a critical annual review. Functional brain imaging shows that the activation of our Lizard Brain interferes with our ability to solve problems or do other cognitive work.[25] So rather than keeping us safe from harm, they can cause unnecessary agitation, undermining our ability to lead well.

Next stop — the Mammalian Brain. Let's imagine that some input is not life-threatening and sashays right past the Lizard Brain and into the Mammalian Brain. This is where our feelings and emotions reside. Like the Lizard Brain, it can be triggered in ways that do not support our best leadership, particularly where our ego is involved. The Mammalian Brain can trigger positive feelings of love and joy. It can also hijack our thinking with anger, fear, jealousy, anxiety, pride, or concern for our status. All of these can cloud our judgment and our ability to lead well.

The Settled Mind: The Prefrontal Cortex

If the mind is settled and able to fully process the input, it will segue to the prefrontal cortex, where a universe of possibilities unfolds. From the prefrontal cortex (also called our *Higher Mind*) we can create, plan, imagine, learn, analyze, ponder, and speak. We experience a playground of infinite options!

Response options:

- *Lizard Brain ➜ Fight / Flight / Freeze*
- *Mammalian Brain ➜ A Handful of Feelings*
- *Higher Mind ➜ Limitless*

Allowing your thoughts to pass safely by your Lizard Brain and your Mammalian Brain enables you to access the wisdom residing in your Higher Mind. Here's the best part: From your prefrontal cortex, you still have access to your instincts, intuition, feelings, and emotions. Only here, however, you get to *choose* how you want to *respond*.

Granted, this entire pathway through the brain takes only a split second with bits of stimuli whizzing through the brain at 250 miles per hour. Still, slowing down and becoming more mindful and intentional will allow your higher mind the opportunity to thoughtfully process input and generally produce far better outcomes.

Don't worry
your Lizard Brain is still ready to jump
in and save the day when it is actually needed.

Between stimulus and response there is a space.
In that space is our power to choose our response.
In our response lies our growth and our freedom.

Viktor Frankl

Allowing Your Mind to Settle

Meditation increases the volume in parts of the brain that regulate emotions and control impulses.[26] As your mind becomes more settled and stable, you are able to observe the inner workings of the mind in real time [27] and thoughtfully choose how best to respond.[28] Rather than obsessively scanning for threats, mindfulness practices allow you to gain perspective and see the world more rationally and in a more positive light.

This week

is dedicated to slowing down in order for your Higher Mind to take the lead. Slowing down allows you to notice when your threat response has been triggered. If you are paying attention, then your body will tell you loud and clear. Notice your heart beating a little faster or your breathing becoming shallow.

This week, we'll practice **NBC**.

Notice - breathe - choose.

Journal Week Three

Even though *it's not life-threatening, my Lizard Brain kicks in when . . .*

And this *causes me to . . .*

Consciously practicing NBC allows me to . . .

So much has been written about gratitude. Decades ago Oprah taught us to keep a gratitude journal. Amazon has more than 3,000 books about gratitude for sale.

We know this stuff already. Why rehash it here?

Amid this growing understanding, a challenge remains. Much of what is out there is about gratitude and about remembering to be grateful. These are worthy endeavors, however, mindfulness has something entirely different to teach us about gratitude.

The Downside of Counting Our Blessings

Each week our church joins in a pastoral prayer that includes a litany of the things we are grateful for: our daily bread, loved ones recovered from illness, blessings of the season. You can feel it wash over the congregation like a soothing balm. When we count our blessings we remind ourselves that we are indeed fortunate. We make a note of how many things are going right—even as some are going wrong. Often we remember to stop and count our blessings when we narrowly avert calamity, when someone we love brushes up against tragedy, or when we witness the deep suffering of others.

We can easily allow our list of gratitudes to become a shield with which we defend ourselves against our most uncomfortable feeling—fear. Often, we count and recount our blessings in order to avoid facing the fear at hand. Standing in stark contrast is ***mindful gratitude***.

Mindful gratitude occurs in this moment—not waiting until evening, or until Sunday service to remember what was noteworthy. Mindfulness awareness brings with it an unfolding sense of awe and wonder, right here, right now. Mindful gratitude is the moment-to-moment awareness of the extraordinariness of absolutely everything and everyone.

By waking up and living mindfully, we can move from counting our blessings to experiencing awe and wonder.

Week 4

Living in Gratitude

Piglet noticed that even though he had a Very Small Heart, it could hold a rather large amount of Gratitude.

A.A. Milne, Winnie-the-Pooh

The moment one gives close attention to anything, even a blade of grass, it becomes a mysterious, awesome, indescribably magnificent world in itself.

Henry Miller

There are only two ways to live your life.

One is as though nothing is a miracle.

The other is as though everything is a miracle.

Albert Einstein

My husband and I are avid backpackers. One recent summer we had been out on the trail for a week eating only dehydrated food. As usual, vivid dreams of fresh, crisp, lettuce, juicy tomatoes, and sweet fruit filled my mind. To our surprise, that day our trail crossed a highway and there stood a small visitor's center. Inside, an angelic volunteer offered fruit to me! I was so excited! She laid a big piece of cantaloupe and a succulent piece of pineapple on a paper towel and handed it to me. Amazed, I thanked her and went outside to eat. When I sat down, I looked down at my paper towel and half the pineapple was missing! Just then I felt myself swallow.

I had missed it.

In leadership retreats we guide participants through a mindfulness meditation with a tangerine. As the fruit sits before them they are asked to explore it as though they have never seen a tangerine before. They study it and notice qualities such as: texture, color, weight, coolness. Then, slowly and deliberately, they inhale the scent, ponder it again, and with intention begin to open it, listening to the sound of the peeling skin. Eventually, mouths watering with anticipation, they bite down on one tiny segment, tasting the tart juice as it squirts between their teeth. They are then invited to eat the entire piece of fruit with the same deliberate intent and presence. Invariably several participants have their minds blown.

A world of experience in one tangerine!

Such is gratitude from a place of mindfulness.

Magnificence is everywhere when we are open to receiving it. For beginners, it's helpful to spend some time in nature (that's a joke—we're all beginners!). Next time you walk somewhere where there are trees, pause and listen: What do you hear? Birds, rustles in the bushes, a plane flying overhead, a dog barking in the distance? Just listen, observe. Nature stirs our sense of awe in the present moment, as does a tangerine, a hot shower, a deep breath—if we are paying attention.

How much pleasure, awe, and gratitude do we miss, simply because our minds are elsewhere?

Freedom From Wanting

One day, when our daughter Gwen was about five years old, she and I were out grocery shopping. As I pushed the cart down the aisle, Gwen picked up a box of Captain Crunch cereal and said to me, "Mommy, I like this." I told her that we were not going to get it and asked her to put it back. She then picked out crackers and, after that, cookies.

As we moved through the market, Gwen continued to reach for this item and that. At one point I turned around to see her walking down the aisle with a bag of marshmallows pressed to her face. She was smelling them, and I could hear her muffled voice, "Oh, I like these. I like these." Again, I had her put them back—and so it went. When we got to the register the same scenario was repeated with a chocolate bar. Exasperated, I barked for her to put it back. She looked at me, shook her head a little and said gently, "Mommy I didn't ask you to buy it. I just said I like it."

The Light Went On

Liking is not the same as wanting.

We can stop at liking! Gwen and I went back that day and together enjoyed smelling the marshmallows. They do smell divine!

When we live mindfully, we get to like things and people. We get to enjoy them, admire them, and appreciate them. We get to ***love*** deeply ***without needing to have them for our own***.

The Downside of Adapting

Human beings are quite adaptable creatures.

And that's a good thing—mostly.

Given a little time, we can adjust to almost anything life tosses our way: financial fluctuations, job changes, and the limitations of aging. We can even recover from unspeakable pain, trauma, and grief. After a time, we are able to see and appreciate the beauty in the world again—maybe just for a moment at first, but before long those moments grow, and life begins to move forward again.

The interesting part is that we not only adapt to the difficulties life throws us—we adapt to the good stuff too!

We all do it. We long for that event, relationship, or position, perhaps seeking after it for years, even decades—and when it finally arrives, there's often great celebration. Champagne corks fly with smiles and laughter all around, but because we're such adaptable creatures, this life worth celebrating quickly morphs into the "new normal" and we begin pursuing the next thing that will REALLY make us happy. Psychologists call the tendency to adapt to the good stuff the **Hedonic Treadmill**.

It's the same in the corporate world. Before the ink is dry on Q1's hefty profits, management is instilling fear in the troops about Q2; a leader forgets to appreciate and thank her trusted admin for years. The team makes a near-impossible ship date by pulling lots of overtime, and then overtime becomes part of the success recipe. In business, the Hedonic Treadmill shows up as, "What have you done for me lately?"

The things we obsess about acquiring today are the very things we take for granted tomorrow.

This week

We practice simple, moment-to-moment appreciation of life, exactly the way it is. We nurture our sense of awe. We focus on noticing without needing to possess. We intentionally celebrate all that is right, without looking down the road at the next challenge. We allow the sublime nature of creation to show itself without needing to do anything but appreciate it.

Journal Week Four

Today I looked at ______________________ *as if for the first time.*

Here is what I noticed . . .

By not paying attention, *I often miss out on the pleasure of . . .*

In my life, *how do I see "wanting" causing me to suffer?*

Thinking about *my direct reports, my team members, my own manager, and the people I am matrixed to, what about each of them can I appreciate? How can I express that to them?*

What do I appreciate *about my employer? My role?*

Week 5

Accepting What Is

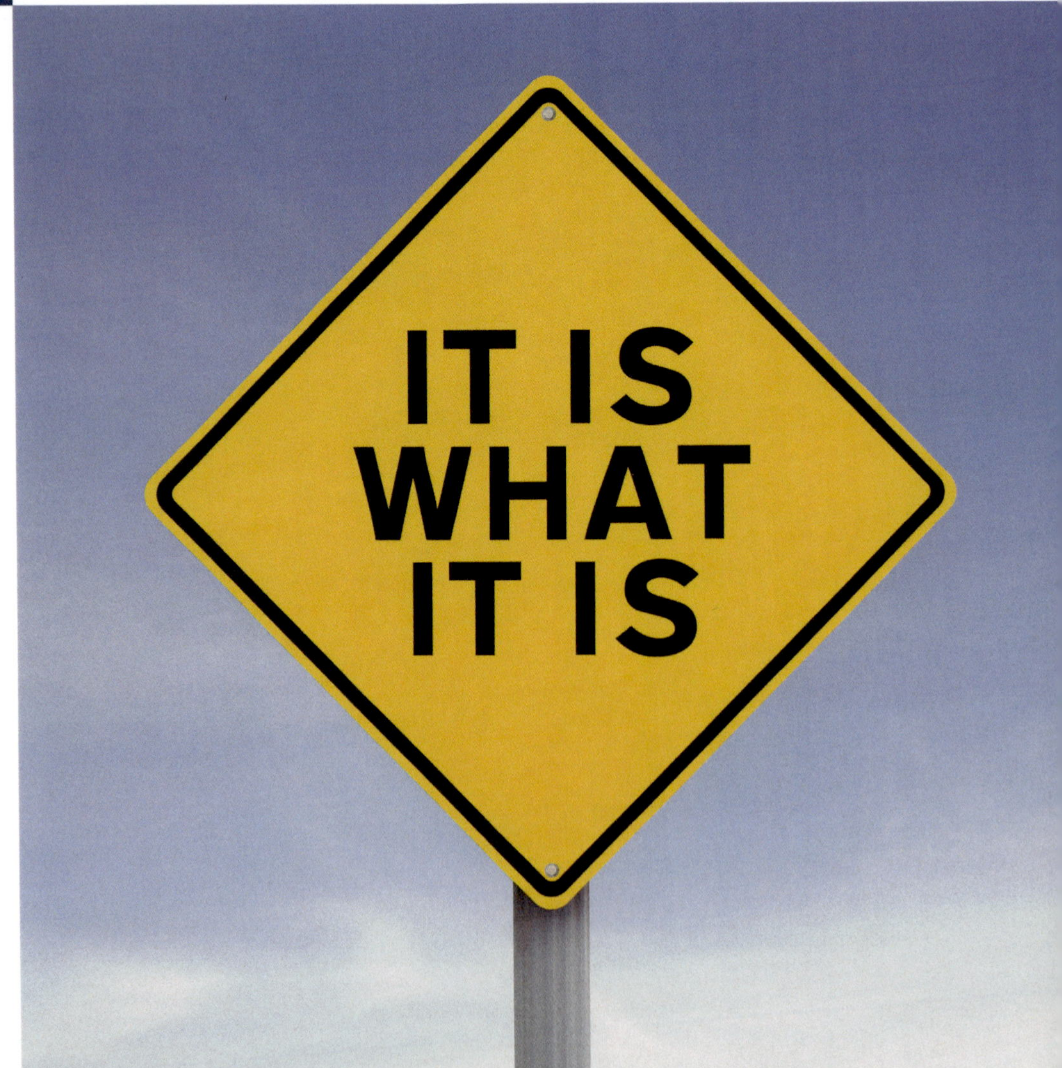

As I was listening to public radio one evening, the host was interviewing a rabbi about the classic question, apropos of a recent natural disaster—How could a loving God let such an event happen to us? The rabbi's response really stuck with me. He answered, "God put us in a physical world, and we are subject to its physical laws. It's not for us to ask why these things happen, but rather to ask,

What now, shall I do?

One of the human brain's favorite pastimes is making up stories, explanations, or contriving meaning for things that happen to us. For any question, one can postulate innumerable answers, all of which may be true. And it's possible, none of them are.

You could ask yourself the question,
"Why was I not offered the promotion?"

You could then make up any of the following answers:

"Someone else was a better fit for the position."

"They thought I was more valuable in my current position."

"It's politics."

"I flubbed the interview."

"I am not good enough/not old enough/too old/not experienced enough/not smooth enough."

"I'm meant to do something else."

"I intimidated the hiring manager with my awesomeness."

Maybe someone didn't like you. Maybe they were intimidated. Maybe there was someone better. Maybe you were meant to do something else. Even if you get feedback from the hiring manager, providing useful pointers for your next swing at a promotion, there is only one fact that matters: You didn't get the promotion. Postulating won't change that so...

Accept what is.

So often the brain hijacks the situation and runs with it, creating reasons, explanations, even recriminations, justifications, etc., none of which are useful. With mindfulness, you can identify that your brain (your ego) is driving all this chatter.

Mindfulness affords the opportunity to approach this question with deep personal integrity. When you "sink into" a state of mindfulness, and check in with what you feel—what's deeply true for you, a clear answer can arise, even if the answer is "Now's not the time to do anything about this." It's OK to revisit the question again and again—just listening—until the answer emerges. Along with or in lieu of an answer, some authentic feelings may emerge: sadness or grief, relief, maybe fear—something deeper and more real than a story.

Be With What Is

Consider how much energy you spend (waste) on figuring out why things happen the way they do. Why your marriage ended, why someone you love died, why your parents treated you the way they did, why you can't seem to stop doing ___, how you screwed up to make your kids the way they are… any troubling question, really.

Pick a big question you have

… like any of the ones above. Just make sure it's a troubling question—something you have struggled with. Write down the first answer that comes to you. After you finish the answer, come up with another answer that makes sense, that could be true, even if you yourself don't believe it. Continue until you have at least five explanations or more if you want.

Can you prove any of the answers?

Can you disprove any?

If all or none are true, what's the difference?

Next, sit in meditation with the question, and let the answers you came up with float by like so many clouds crossing the horizon, and return to your breath ongoingly. Then consider an action or attitude you can adopt that makes sense, that gives you a sense of both peace and power.

Serenity

The classic Serenity Prayer shows what this looks like: "Grant me the serenity to accept the things I cannot change, the courage to change the things I can, and the wisdom to know the difference."

When you bring your challenges to meditation, you can achieve all the aims outlined in the Serenity Prayer—that serenity, that courage, that wisdom.

Not taking yourself personally

In Don Miguel Ruiz' famous book, *The Four Agreements*, the second agreement is not to take anything personally. This includes yourself. Think of an area of your life where you are suffering, perhaps an area where you have been wronged by another or by an organization, or a recent loss. Imagine another person in another part of the country, another city, who had the same thing happen to them. Of course, a person like that exists, and it's just as real for them as it is for you. But, do you need to take on their suffering? Of course not, even as awful as it is.

Likewise, you have the choice—on a moment-to-moment basis—to not "take on" what just happened to you. This is not the same as suppressing your feelings—which is not accepting what is—but rather not making up stories about what should have happened, what might have happened, what it means, the "if-only," etc.

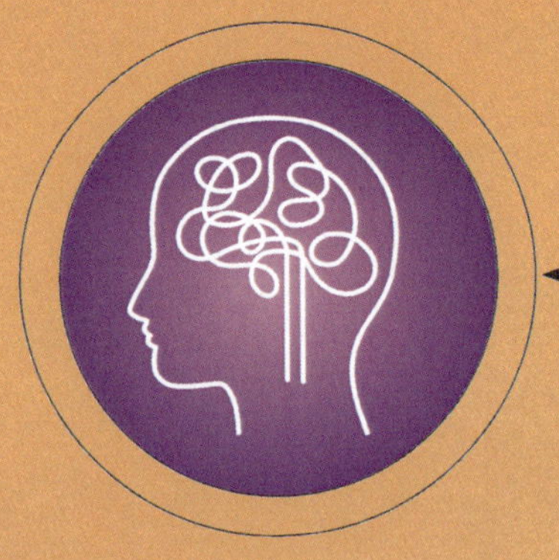

Consider the mindless response

I just got in a car accident. %@#$! It was my fault. My insurance is going to go up. My neck hurts. %@#$! Did I hurt the other guy? I AM SO SCREWED! I should not have followed so closely. %@#$.

Consider the mindful response

I just got in a car accident, and I was at fault. I am scared. %@#$! I'm worried. %@#$! That's OK. ***What, now, shall I do?*** OK, breathe. Get out of traffic... Is it safe? Call my admin. Call a tow truck. Get insurance info out.. Breathe... This is going to be OK. This happens to everyone at some point. It's OK.

To have a mindful response when crisis hits is the hallmark of a strong leader. Some might say it takes "mental toughness," and that may be true, but really, it just takes being mindful, accepting what is, and constantly course-correcting yourself when your Lizard Brain is going nuts.

This week

we focus on acceptance of ourselves and our situation. We notice when we are telling ourselves, *"If only _____, then ______ would have happened."* We remind ourselves that to be human is to have setbacks, to grieve, to feel, to celebrate, and that these things say nothing about our worthiness or qualifications. We consider that the question to ask is not *"Why,"* or *"What does it mean,"* but *"What, now, shall I do."* And sometimes, the answer is *"Nothing."*

A man went into a tailor's shop

... to buy his first custom made suit. After hearing what it would cost the man said, "Oh no. I can't pay anywhere near that price." To this the tailor said, "Hmmm, maybe I can help you out. I have this suit over here. A customer paid top dollar to have it made, but then he never came to pick it up. It's been two years, so you can have it cheap."

The customer took a closer look. It was an exquisite suit ... the finest fabric... perfectly made... "Yes, yes," he said, "Let me try it on."

The man tried on the suit, and it was gorgeous. He admired himself in the mirror... But then he noticed that one arm of the jacket was a tad too short. The tailor said, "Ah... that's no problem. Just lift your shoulder up a bit."

The man did as the tailor suggested and raised that shoulder, so it fit in the sleeve.

"See! Now it's perfect." said the tailor.

Then the man noticed it was a bit tight around the middle. He thought, "If I just suck in my stomach a bit... yeah, that'll work."

Then the man noticed that one of the pant legs was a bit long as well. The tailor said, "No worries. Just kick your foot out a little when you walk and it will fall just right as you step."

The man thought, "Yeah. That'll work."

And the man loved the suit so much that he bought it and wore it right out of the tailor's shop.

He was walking along, feeling quite dashing, when two women came walking by him on the street. He saw that they noticed that he was lookin' mighty fine.

After the women passed, one leaned in and said to the other. "Did you see that beautiful suit?"

Her friend replied, "Yeah, nice suit, but too bad about the guy."

Journal Week Five

I want people to think I'm ______________________ .

In order to maintain this image I . . . ______________________

If I were *really myself, I would ...*

What are some *things about my organization that I would like to change, and have the power to influence?*

What are some *things about my organization that I would like to change, but cannot significantly influence?*

If I were *able to let go and accept the things I cannot change about my organization, I ...*

Choosing Happiness

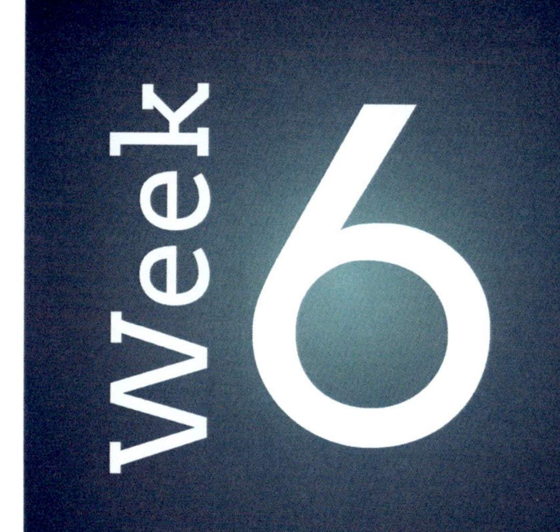

A happy man is too satisfied with the present to dwell too much on the future. Albert Einstein

What makes you happy?

Before reading on, take a moment to write a few things.

Science has important things to teach us about what makes us happy and unhappy.

Researchers from Northwestern University tracked a group of lottery winners and another group of people who had been in debilitating, near-fatal car accidents. As one might expect, just after these significant events the lottery winners reported being happy, and the accident victims reported being unhappy. Two years later the researchers tracked down the same people and reassessed their general level of happiness—with stunning results. The impact from their big life event no longer had any measurable effect on their happiness. People who were happy before were happy again even if they had been among the car accident victims, and the grumpy people, even if they won the lottery, were grumpy again.[29]

The events of our lives cause only blips in our level of happiness and positivity. Then, as discussed earlier, we quickly acclimate and return to our "normal" state. The question becomes, "How can we create a "new normal?"

Answering that question is what this week is all about.

Illusion ONE

If I can arrange the things—and people—in my life to be the way I want them, then I will be happy.

First, the chance that you will get all the things and people in your life to line up to your satisfaction—all at the same time—is highly unlikely. There are simply too many moving parts. And if you did get everything to line up the way you want it, how long would that last? A few minutes maybe? That's a lot of work, and a lot of waiting for a few minutes of bliss.

Illusion TWO

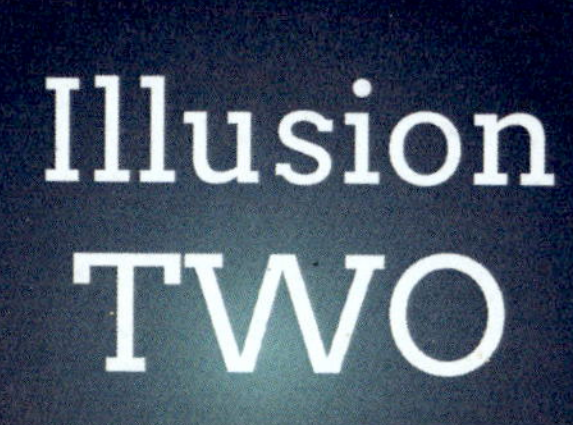

If I work really hard, then I will become successful and that will make me happy.

It's baffling how much staying power this folkloric promise has when it is absolutely false. Success does not lead to happiness. Period. In fact, the opposite is true!

Becoming successful will not—cannot—make you happy. But, happiness will go a long way toward making you more successful. Shawn Achor coined this phenomenon in the *Happiness Advantage.*

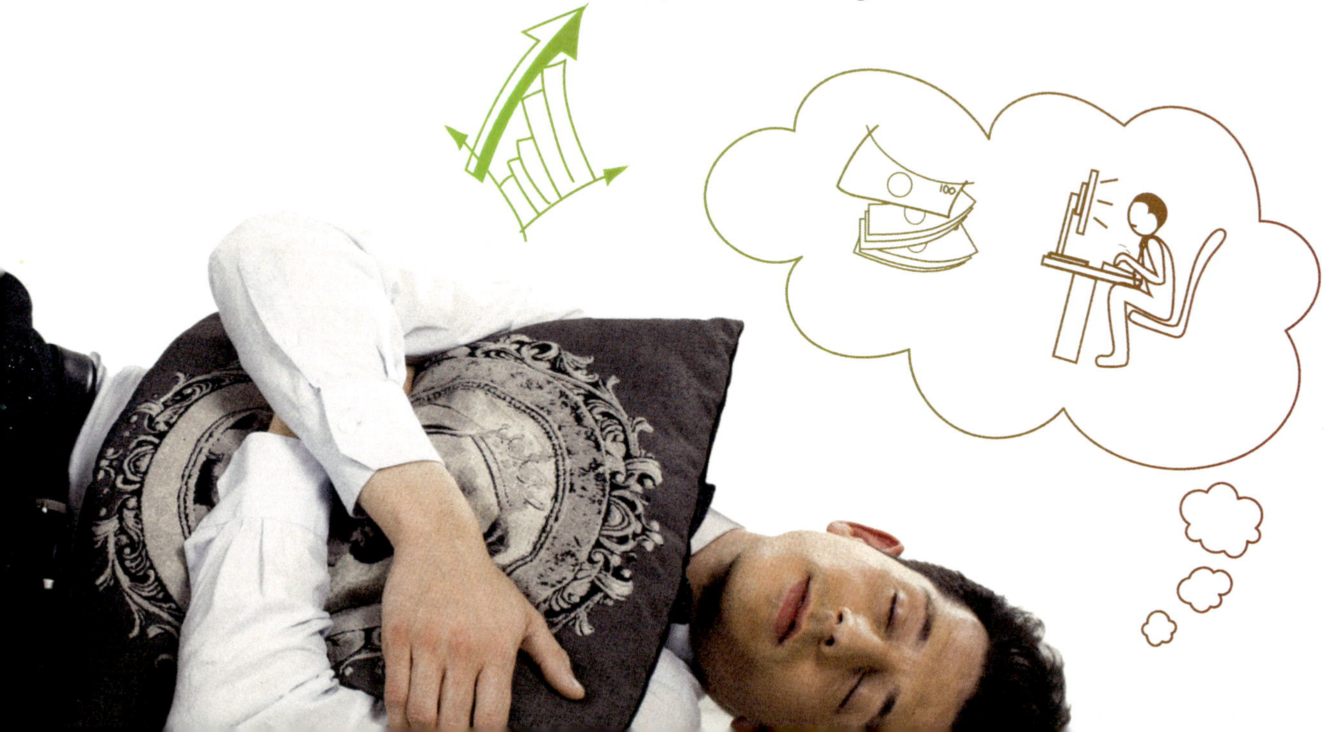

Happiness leads to success in nearly every domain, including work, health, friendship, sociability, creativity, and energy.

Shawn Achor

The Happiness Advantage

Happiness bestows an avalanche of benefits that reach far beyond the pleasure of an elevated mood. Compared to neutral or negative people, happy people:

Make far more money[30]

Get promoted faster[31]

Get sick less often

Get well faster[32]

Cope better with stress and trauma[33]

Have sharper cognitive abilities[34]

Stay married longer[35]

In an elegantly designed study, a group of 180 Catholic nuns were studied to learn about the effects of happiness. This group of women entered a convent nearly 100 years ago while in their late teens and early twenties. As part of their early spiritual development they journaled regularly, creating their own autobiographies. Researchers were able to meticulously study these women's journals and correlate the data with their medical records. Those who were happiest in their twenties lived (on average)10 years longer than the sisters who were least happy.[37]

Happiness leads to a better life in nearly every respect, including leadership. There is plenty of research that shows happy people make better leaders,[38] but I suspect you don't need such proof. If you have ever worked with an unhappy person you know the truth of this all too well. Happy people inspire us to bring our best everyday.

To be clear, we are not talking about acting cheerful or happy. Putting on an act undermines trust and connection, while a genuinely positive outlook improves collaboration, cooperation, productivity, and profit. Trying to fake it can be disastrous.

How to Be Happy

We constantly push happiness over the horizon to some other time and place.

Mountains of evidence point to 2 key ingredients in cultivating a happy life:

Be here now

The harsh truth about happiness is: You will never be happy in the future. Never. It's not even possible. The only time you can ever be happy is right now... and now... and now...

To be happy we need to toss out our "When I... then I..." thinking.

"When I get the promotion, then I will be able to relax and enjoy myself."

"When my company goes public, then I'll be happy."

"When I get X job..."

"When I get married..."

"When I get divorced..."

"When we get our kids through school..."

"When I retire..."

Love

In the largest longitudinal study ever undertaken, the Harvard Men's Study (aka The Grant Study) followed a group of students beginning in 1938. Over the course of 75 years, teams of researchers gathered staggering amounts of data on 268 men. Dr. George Vaillant directed the study for 30 years ending in 2004.[39]
In his book, Vaillant writes, "The seventy-five years and twenty million dollars expended on the Grant Study points... to a straightforward five-word conclusion:

Happiness is love.

Full stop.

This week

→ our mindfulness practice focuses on cultivating our own happiness. If that feels selfish, then you should know that happy people contribute far more to their communities, their work, and their families. Your happiness is your gift to the world and to those you love. This week, look for happiness exactly where you are—in this moment, in this place. Call into suspicion any thought that you will be happier at some point in the future—especially if it means sacrificing a bunch of present moments to get there.

During this week's meditation, we will intentionally nurture our own happiness by increasing our capacity to love and to connect with others.

Journal Week Six

What *makes you happy? (Consider the things that bring you joy, rather than the absence of things that cause you stress.)*

I am or was *most happy when...*

The things *I think need to happen before I can be really happy are...*

As a leader *in my organization, cultivating more love would cause me to...*

Who benefits *most (besides you) when you are happy...*

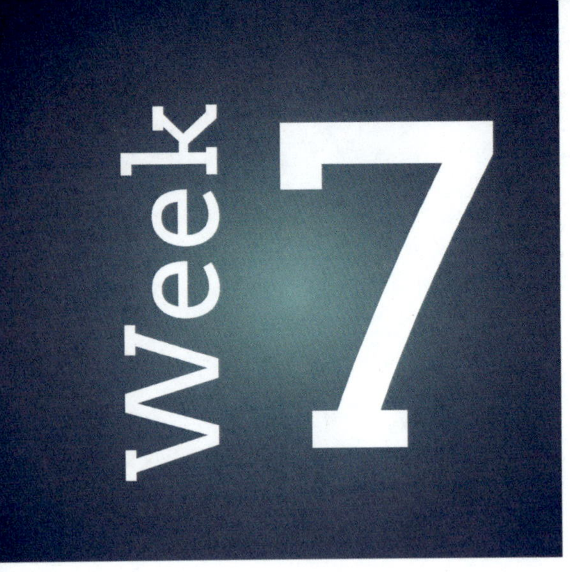

When I was a child my mother said to me, 'If you become a soldier, you'll be a general. If you become a monk, you'll be the pope.' Instead I became a painter and wound up as Picasso.

Pablo Picasso

If Friday rolls around and you find yourself thinking, "TGIF," it's likely that you haven't found your fire yet.

When you wake up and think "TGIM," you're there!

Fewer than 20 percent of leaders have a strong sense of their own individual purpose.[40] When we lack a clear purpose, we continue to follow the path of least resistance, choosing within safe and known boundaries—accepting jobs, partners, and spouses mostly because they showed up at the right time. While each choice you make might seem like the best option at the time, the end result is a life you have never powerfully chosen for yourself. Your life just kind of "happened."

There is another finer and more purposeful way to live. To begin, you'll need to

find your fire!

To be nobody but yourself in a world which is doing its best, night and day, to make you everybody else, means to fight the hardest battle which any human being can fight; and never stop fighting.

E.E. Cummings

Find
Your
Fire

The two most important days in your life are the day you are born and the day you find out why.
— *Mark Twain*

Finding your fire is a life-sized journey. While exploring our gifts and passions can be fun, even exhilarating, stepping into our most brilliant, happy, passionate life presents us with a minefield to dance through! That inner roommate of yours will undoubtedly have much to say. If you are like most of us, every time you begin to dream, your inner critic will become alarmed, even throwing a tantrum, insisting that you absolutely have to stay exactly where and how you are.

Remember your inner roommate? *He or she will say anything to keep you in your "comfort zone," no matter how uncomfortable you have become with your status quo. He or she will remind you of:*

- *All your obligations*
- *What you "should" be and do*
- *All the people you may disappoint if you change course*
- *The risks and all that could go wrong*
- *How embarrassing failure would be*
- *How silly you are to consider things so far beyond your reach*
- *How pursuing a different path might mean you'll no longer compare as favorably to others*

For most of us, the inner critic keeps the constant drumbeat within the mind, "You're just not good enough to have what you really want."

To find your fire you will need to face your fears—one by one—and find what lies beneath them—until you unveil your brilliant truth. With a settled mind, you can get to the real fears that stand in your way and choose to act in courage toward an outcome you really want.

Ask yourself: *"What would I do if I were not afraid?" "What would I do if I knew I could not fail?"* When you decide that your fear, vis-a-vis your internal critic, will no longer be calling the shots

magic happens.

At the Gettysburg Address, Abraham Lincoln honored the fallen soldiers. He said of these heros that they gave their last "full measure of devotion."

What is worthy of your devotion?

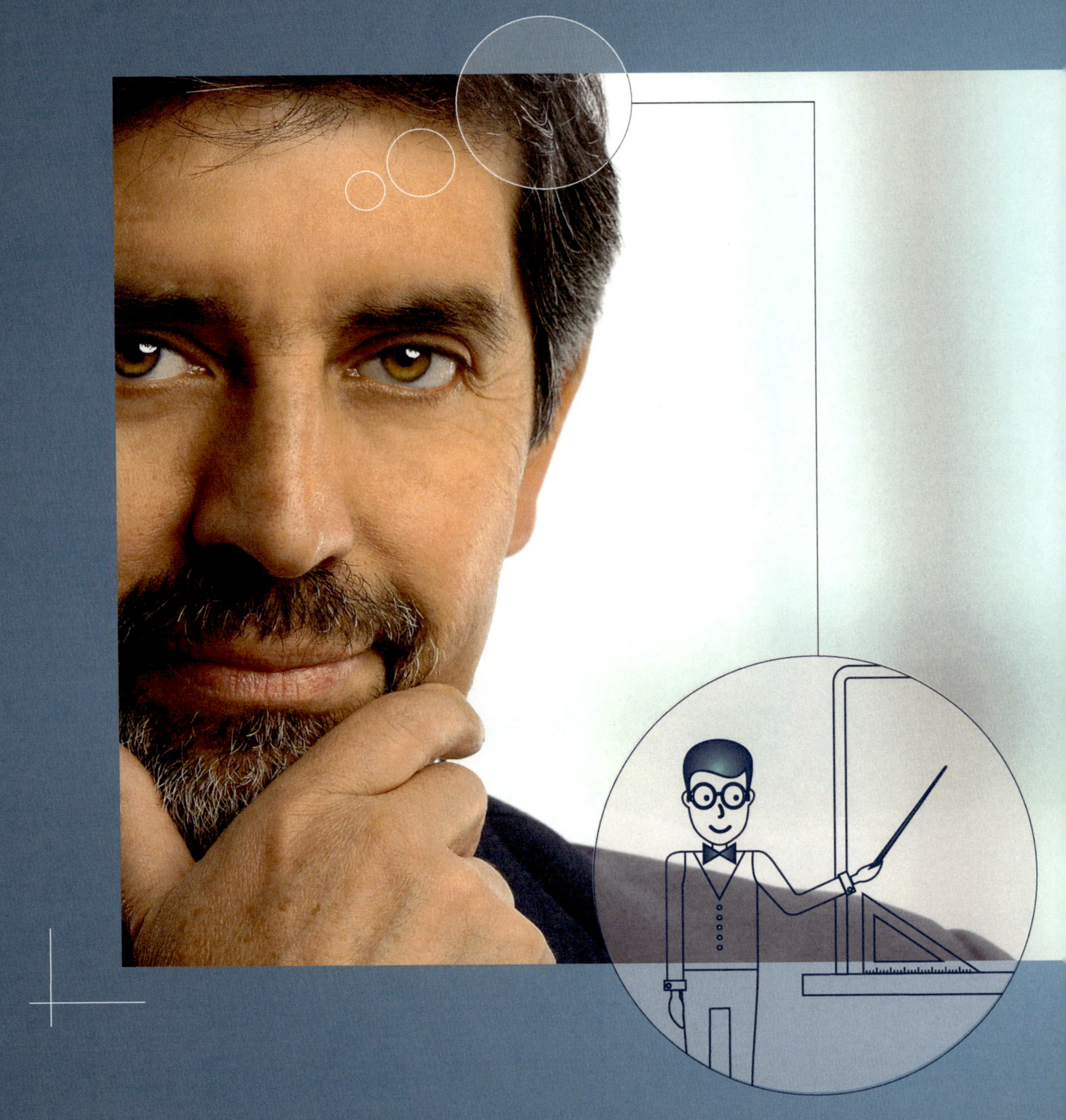

Carlos

was a 49-year-old director in a large corporation who was being groomed for the executive suite.

During one of our coaching sessions I asked him, "Where do you see yourself in five years?".

He quickly replied, "Retired!"

"Really?!?!" In a stumbling moment as his coach, I could not contain my surprise. Carlos had the kind of job everyone wants: autonomy, interesting work, generous compensation, and a promising future.

"Why?" I asked. "What do you want to do when you retire?"

"I want to be a teacher."

"Who do you want to teach?" I asked.

"I don't know. Teenagers maybe or junior high kids. Maybe even community college."

"What do you want to teach?"

"I think I'd like to try my hand at teaching US History, or Political Science—but my background is in math, so maybe I'll need to start there."

The truth was, Carlos really didn't care what he taught or whom he taught. He simply longed to teach. Unfortunately, he was far from the classroom. To Carlos, his enviable position was little more than a path that would someday lead out of corporate America and into a classroom.

Though Carlos had discovered the work that deserved his full measure of devotion, he was convinced that it lay on the other side of retirement.

Coaching opened Carlos' eyes to the possibility of fulfilling his passion within his current organization. Facing his fears head-on, Carlos approached the CEO offering his skills as a teacher coupled with his his deep knowledge of the organization. As a result, Carlos now leads the training arm of his company! Carlos found his fire and ignited it right where he was! He wakes up each Monday thinking: TGIM!

Imagine you are walking into a large meeting hall, filled with hundreds of people. You take a seat and notice a person walking up to the podium. This person begins to talk and the audience becomes quiet, leaning in with rapt attention. During the talk, the crowd is moved again and again—to laughter, to knowing nods, and a few tender tears. As this person finishes speaking the crowd leaps to their feet for a standing ovation. The speaker has rocked their world.

This speaker is you *at some point in the not-too-distant future. What did you share with the audience that day? What did you talk about? What moved them so?*

By and large a good rule for finding out is this: The kind of work God usually calls you to is the kind of work that you need most to do and the world most needs to have done. The place God calls you to is the place where your deep gladness and the world's deep hunger meet.

Frederick Buechner

Take a few slow, deep breaths.

Ask yourself: *Where does my deep gladness meet the needs of the world?*

Even if you're not yet clear about that—what do you know? Where do you find your deepest gladness? (Don't ask yourself HOW just yet. Asking HOW too early shuts down possibilities.)

Most of us go to our graves with our music still inside us, unplayed.
Oliver Wendell Holmes

What

is the music inside you?

This week

we shine a light in the corners of the mind to see what gifts you have hidden away. You will be invited to explore your passions, your "deep gladness" and the music inside you that longs to be played.

Before we go there, ask yourself, "Who in my life (____________________) has always recognized my gifts and abilities, maybe even better than I have? Consider asking them to help you hold yourself accountable.

Journal Week Seven

When I was 10, *before the world told me I couldn't, I wanted to be a...*

The truth *I am ready to see is...*

In what surprising ways,

or even odd places, do I find joy?

Have a conversation

with someone you know, outside of work, and ask them what kind of work would be most deeply fulfilling to them. Then answer this:

What magic might occur if I had this conversation with everyone on my team?

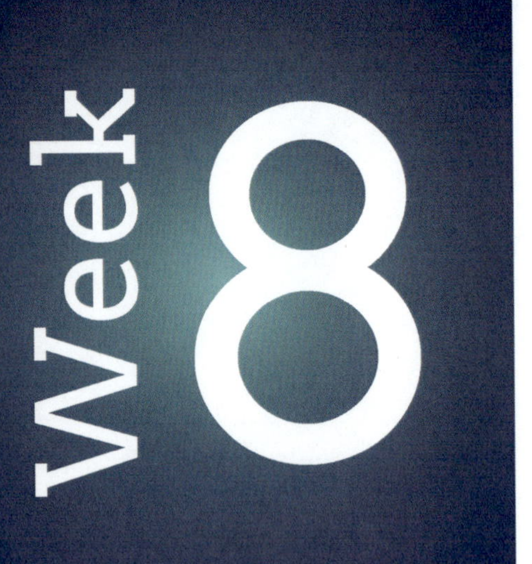

Moving Beyond Our Stories

Besides opposable thumbs, perhaps the most remarkable thing that

> *God has given you one face,*
> *and you make yourself another.*
> William Shakespeare

separates humans from other creatures is our ability to

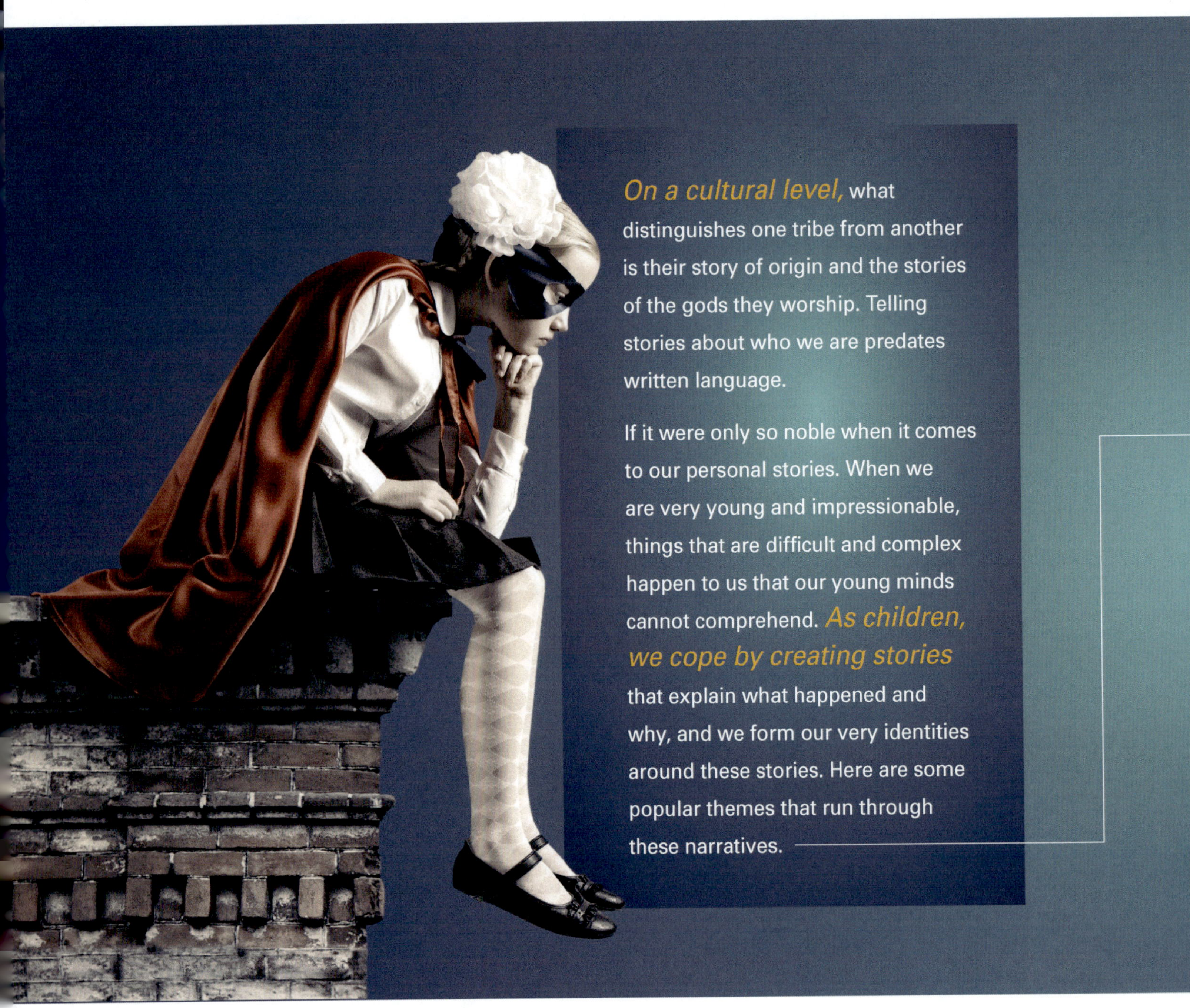

On a cultural level, what distinguishes one tribe from another is their story of origin and the stories of the gods they worship. Telling stories about who we are predates written language.

If it were only so noble when it comes to our personal stories. When we are very young and impressionable, things that are difficult and complex happen to us that our young minds cannot comprehend. *As children, we cope by creating stories* that explain what happened and why, and we form our very identities around these stories. Here are some popular themes that run through these narratives.

Stories about who and how we are

I am not accepted for who I am.
In order to get, I have to give.
What I do matters more than who I am.
Something is missing from my life.
My life is harsh and difficult.

I can't trust anyone.
I am frustrated by limitations; I want it all.
I cannot be vulnerable; it isn't safe.
In order to belong, I have to fit in.

Stories that make us feel special

I am a fan of this team.
I believe in the God of this religion.
I own these things.
I am the boss.
I eat only this, and not that.
I'm deep.
I am a member of this political party.

I am in recovery.
I am self-made.
I am patriotic.
I stand for this principle.
I am my cool Facebook persona.
I am a survivor.
I am a man, or a woman, a wife, husband, mother, father, etc.

Feel familiar?

These stories shape how we see ourselves, for better or for worse—often for worse. When we line up our stories with facts, they become ridiculous. We cherry-pick the facts that support our story, while we ignore a drawer full of facts that support alternate takes on our lives. Once we settle on a story theme that works for us, we use that theme as a filter for the facts that support our self-concept—long after that coping mechanism has outlived its usefulness.

Take, for instance, the story I have about my ability to travel as much as I'd like:

I'll never be able to travel much because I can't take the time off, I don't have the cash flow, and I don't have the freedom.

I might back up my story with the following supporting evidence or "facts"

I only get two weeks of vacation in my current position, and that's simply not enough.

A trip to India, Japan, Peru, or Australia would cost a small fortune.

Even if I could get the time off, my department would be a mess when I got back.

I have to wait until I retire to travel.

However, anyone who has traveled much knows that millions of people who travel do not live according to this evidence. They have stories that allow them to travel:

Their facts might look more like this

More and more companies offer their employees unlimited time off.

Travel can be expensive or cheap—the choice is mine.

The world doesn't revolve around me or my team. By properly training my team, I can vanish for awhile and it will be alright.

If something really matters to me, I get it done, no matter what.

We can't help but make up stories.

Our brains are designed to do it.

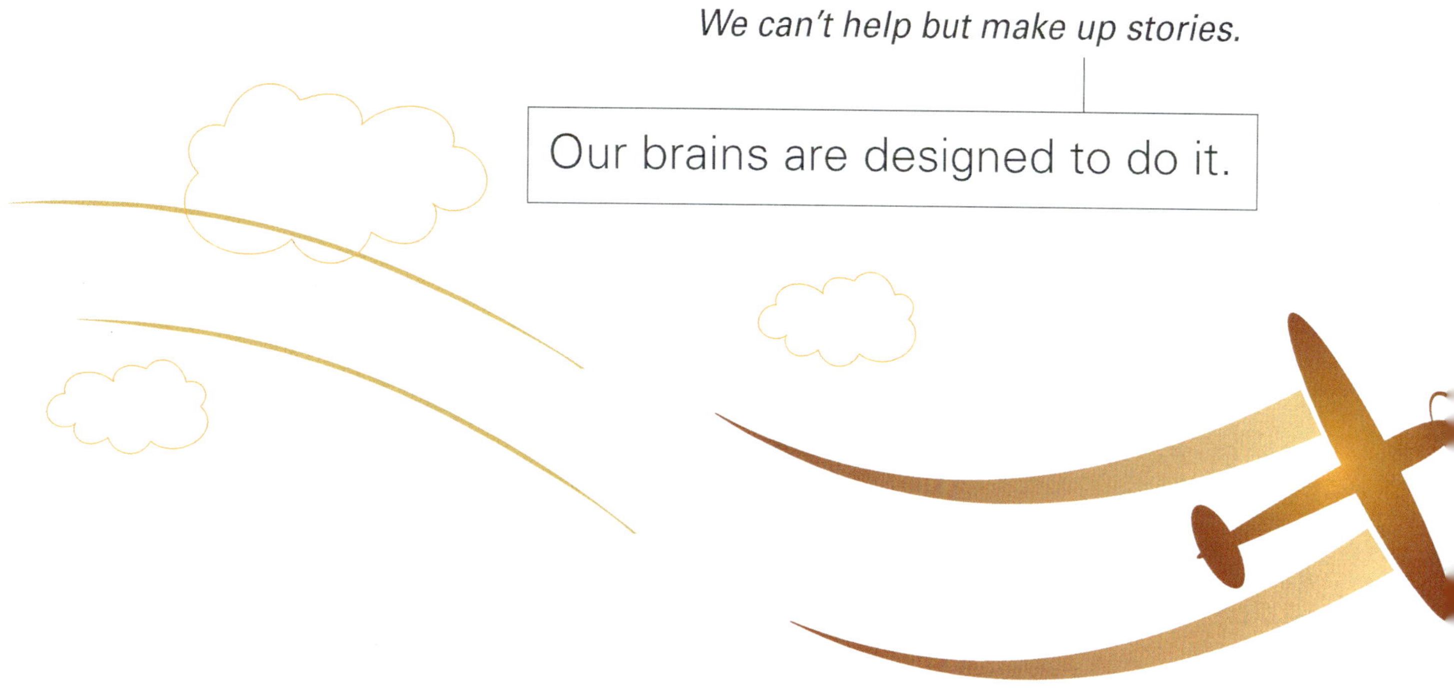

Fortunately *we have an amazing human capacity,* **the ability to**

After all, what is a story, if not a collection of thoughts and feelings regarding a particular subject? In mindfulness, we practice being present to thoughts and feelings without clinging to them.

We notice them, then let them go.

I once participated in a personal growth weekend where we took a deep dive into our stories. Each person wrote down a couple of pages, in excruciating detail, a story about something in their life that was frustrating them or causing them pain. Then each person paired up with another and took turns reading their story aloud, over and over and over and over and over again, until they finally got tired of telling their story. At the end of the exercise, everyone in the room was sick of their story and ready to move on.

Some stories are empowering, yet even empowering stories can keep us in a holding pattern, limiting our ability to continually grow. Most of our stories bind and limit us—in other words, by believing in or indulging our own stories, we pigeonhole ourselves.

let go of our stories.

Now you may be asking

If I am not the sum of my stories:

You are the awareness that sits behind all those stories, struggles, and successes. You are pure consciousness. To live in that awareness can be the most freeing feeling you have ever known.

That's the real you.

Practicing mindfulness is the real-world way to let go of our stories. Mindfulness is not denying or forgetting, but rather untethering yourself from all the stories you have collected over the years, and showing up as simply you.

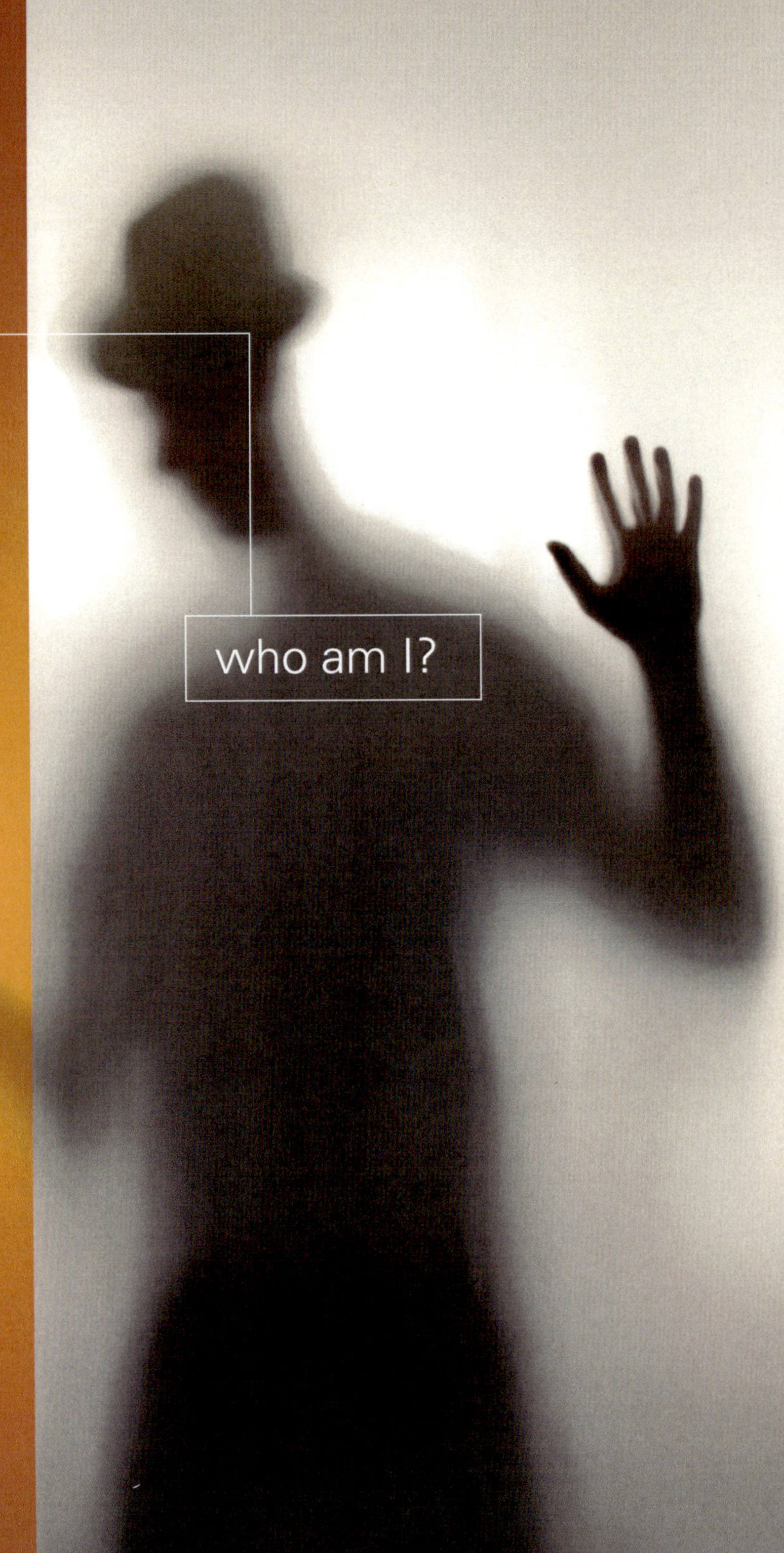

Journal Week Eight

What stories *positive or negative—do I have about where I work?*

What stories *do I have about myself and the people I work with?*

Implications for Leadership

The stakes can be high: You can have a positive story about a particular employee, perhaps begun by a good first impression or an early win on an important project. However, unless you drop that story, you may be blind to serious performance or behavior issues that others might notice. Likewise, someone with whom you "got off on the wrong foot" with might actually be a powerful ally if you're able to let the bad first impression go and start from scratch.

Dropping our story gives us access to what's known in Zen Buddhism as

beginner's eyes.

Like a beginner or a child, we enter situations with eagerness and wonder, with a lack of preconceptions or self-limitations.

What does it look like?

While dropping our stories and living in the present feels like waking up *to you,* to those around you, it looks like

humility.

The stories about yourself that you hope will impress people, may indeed impress them. Your background, credentials, and experiences may convey a sense of importance. Unfortunately, they can also become obstacles to connecting and building relationships.

When leaders let their identity stories fall away, people are naturally drawn to them—they are what we call *charismatic.* An awakened leader has nothing to project, protect, nor prove. We reveal our true selves by being fully present with those around us. Awakened leaders show up only as themselves: their brilliant, quirky, sometimes messy, real selves. It is this humility—rather than a projected sense of importance—that inspires devotion (job performance) from team members.

This week

We anchor all of our experiences in the present. On a large piece of paper, write in big letters, "This moment matters!" and post it where you will see it often. Let it be a chorus that plays in your head continuously throughout the week, because...

this moment does matter.

and now this one...

and now this one...

All the weeks to come

Your lifetime homework is to wake-up and to keep waking up again and again. When you realize you have drifted into mindlessness (whether it's been a minute or a decade), come back to yourself.

Come back to your senses:
See. Hear. Feel.
And rejoice...

because you are awake once again.

Final Thoughts

Congratulations on completing The Snow Globe Effect.

Over these weeks, you have undertaken the important work of training your mind to observe your own consciousness and to focus with intention. Each time you sat to meditate, another more subtle change was taking place at the same time: You were shifting your relationship with TIME.

Our world has become hooked on the need for speed. As a culture, we are losing our patience. We hate to wait.

According to Google research, even a five second wait for a website to load is long enough to make us hit the <BACK button. Giant retailers battle it out for same-day delivery supremacy. In some cities, shoppers can place an order and have it on their doorstep in a few hours. Dating apps instantly deliver prospects to our phone screens. We no longer mix and mingle with strangers to meet potential dates.

And life whizzes by at warp speed.

Today's frenetic pace makes cultivating mindfulness challenging, yet ever more critical.

By now, you know mindfulness improves the *quality* of life. It can seem to increase the *quantity* as well. Time slows down, allowing you to fully inhabit each moment—each hour—each year of the one precious life you have been given.

What a gift!

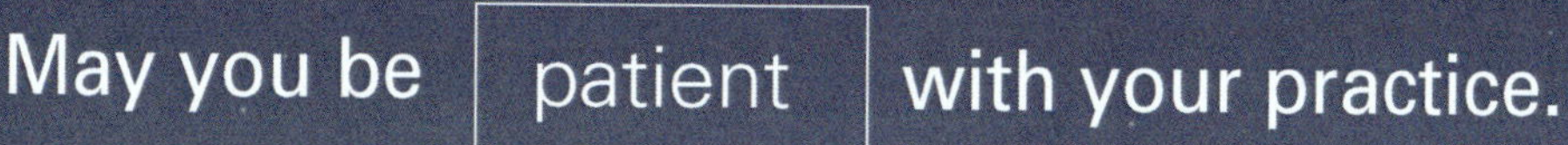

May you be patient with your practice.

May you be kind to yourself.

May you see ever more clearly,

as the days and years go by.

End Notes

1. The Hay Group. Coercive Style of Leadership. New Delhi /Mumbai: The Hay Group, 2012. Print
2. Gilbert, Daniel, and Matthew A. Killingsworth. "A Wandering Mind Is an Unhappy Mind." Science Magazine, 10 Nov. 2010. Web.
3. Ibid.
4. Wolkin, Jennifer R. "Cultivating Multiple Aspects of Attention through Mindfulness Meditation Accounts for Psychological Well-Being through Decreased Rumination." The Journal of Psychology Research and Behavior Management, vol. 8, June 2015, pp. 171–180.
5. Gilbert, Daniel, and Matthew A. Killingsworth. "A Wandering Mind Is an Unhappy Mind." Science Magazine, 10 Nov. 2010. Web.
6. Traditionally attributed to the Buddha.
7. Williams, Ray. "Why 'Doing Nothing' Improves Productivity and Well Being." Psychology Today 9 Nov. 2016: n. pag. Web.
8. Mann, Charles Riborg. A Study of Engineering and Education. Vol. 11. Boston: Merrymount, 1918. Print.
9. Goleman, Daniel. Emotional Intelligence. London: Bloomsbury, 2014. Print.
10. Ruderman, M. N., and K. Hunnam. "Leadership Skills and Emotional Intelligence (Unpublished Manuscript)." Center for Creative Leadership 2001: n. pag. S. Web. 12 Nov. 2017.
11. Cherniss, Cary. "Business Case for Emotional Intelligence." Consortium for Research on Emotional Intelligence in Organizations. Graduate School of Applied and Professional Psychology, 1999. Web.
12. Hogan, Robert, and Robert B. Kaiser. "Management Derailment: Personality Assessment and Mitigation." American Psychological Association Handbook of Industrial and Organizational Psychology. By Joyce Hogan. Washington DC: American Psychological Association, 2014. N. pag. 106 Print.
13. Adkins, Amy. "The State of the American Manager: Analytics and Advice for Leaders "Business Journal (2015): n. pag. Gallup. Web.
14. Kabat-Zinn, Jon. Full Catastrophe Living: Using the Wisdom of Your Body and Mind to Face Stress, Pain, and Illness; the Mindfulness-based Stress Reduction (MBSR) Program Used in Medical Centers Worldwide. New York, NY: Bantam, 2013. Print.
15. Hoge, Elizabeth A, and Maxine M. Chen. "Loving-Kindness Meditation Practice Associated with Longer Telomeres in Women." Brain, Behavior and Immunity: The Journal of Psychoneuro-immunology Research Society, vol. 32, Aug. 2013, pp. 159–163.
16. Johnson, Susan K. Consciousness and Cognition 19.2 (2010): 597-605. Web. 12 Nov. 2017.
17. Thaddeus W. Pace, and Lobsang T. Negi, Phd. "Effect of Compassion Meditation on Neuro-endocrine, Innate Immune and Behavioral Responses to Psychosocial Stress." Journal of Psychoneuroendocrinology 34.1 (2009): 87-98. Web. 12 Nov. 2017.
18. Zeidan, F. C. "Brain Mechanisms Supporting Modulation of Pain by Mindfulness Meditation." US National Library of Medicine National Institutes of Health. PMC, 6 Apr. 2011. Web. 12 Nov. 2017.
19. Davidson, Richard J, et al. "Alterations in Brain and Immune Function Produced by Mindfulness Meditation." Psychosomatic Medicine 65.4 (2003): 564-70. Web.

20. Tang, Y.-Y, et al. "Short-term Meditation Training Improves Attention and Self-regulation." Proceedings of the National Academy of Sciences 104.43 (2007): 17152-7156. Web.

21.. Sapolsky, Robert M. Why Zebras Don't Get Ulcers: An Updated Guide to Stress, Stress-related Diseases, and Coping. New York: W.H. Freeman, 1998. Print.

22. Ibid.

23. Woollett, Katherine J. "Talent in the Taxi: A Model System for Exploring Expertise." Royal Society Publishing, 12 Apr. 2009.

24. Hammerness, Paul, and Margaret Moore. "Train Your Brain To Focus." Harvard Business Review (2012): n. pag. Web.

25. Ibid.

26. Cromie, William J. "Meditation Found to Increase Brain Size: Mental Calisthenics Bulk up Some Layers." Http://news.harvard.edu/gazette/story/2006/02/meditation-found-to-increase-brain-size/. Harvard Gazette, 2 Feb. 2006. Web. 12 Nov. 2017. Web.

27. Sze, Jocelyn A., et al. "Coherence between Emotional Experience and Physiology: Does Body Awareness Training Have an Impact?" Emotion 10.6 (2010): 803-14. Web.

28. Jazaieri, Hooria, et al. "A Randomized Controlled Trial of Compassion Cultivation Training: Effects on Mindfulness, Affect, and Emotion Regulation." Motivation and Emotion 38.1 (2013): 23-35. Web.

29. Brickman, Philip, and Dan Coates. "Lottery Winners and Accident Victims: Is Happiness Relative?" Journal of Personality and Social Psychology, vol. 36, no. 8, 1978, pp. 917–927.

30. Vaillant, George E. Triumphs of Experience: The Men of the Harvard Grant Study. Cambridge (Massachusetts): Belknap of Harvard UP, 2012. Print.

31. Pryce-Jones, Jessica. Happiness at Work: Maximizing Your Psychological Capital for Success. Oxford: Wiley-Blackwell, 2010. Print.

32. Vedhara, K., et al. "Coping Style and Depression Influence the Healing of Diabetic Foot Ulcers: Observational and Mechanistic Evidence." Diabetologia 53.8.

33. Kabat-Zinn, Jon. Full Catastrophe Living: Using the Wisdom of Your Body and Mind to Face Stress, Pain, and Illness; the Mindfulness-based Stress Reduction (MBSR) Program Used in Medical Centers World-wide. New York, NY: Bantam, 2013. Print.

34. Alice Isen. "An Influence of Positive Affect on Decision Making in Complex Situations: Theoretical Issues With Practical Implications." Journal of Consumer Psychology, 11.2 (n.d.): 75-85. Web. 12 Nov. 2017.

35. Luhmann, M., et al. "Subjective Well-Being and Adaptation to Life Events: A Meta-Analysis." Journal of Personality and Social Psychology (2011): Web.

36. Gallagher, Winfred. Rapt: Attention and the Focused Life. N.p.: Penguin Group, 2010. Print.

37. Danner, et al. Positive Emotions in Early Life and Longevity: Findings from the Nun Study. University of Kentucky, n.d. Web. 2001.

38. "Special Issue: Leadership and Emotions, Is a Happy Leader a Good Leader? A Meta-analytic Investigation of Leader Trait Affect and Leadership." The Leadership Quarterly 26.4 (2015): 557-76. Web.

39. Vaillant, George E. Triumphs of Experience: The Men of the Harvard Grant Study. Cambridge, MA: Belknap of Harvard UP, 2015. Print.

40. Craig, Nick . "From Purpose to Impact." Harvard Business Review (2014): 98-106. Print

About the Authors

Lydia Richards is an executive coach, speaker, and facilitator serving corporate clients throughout the United States from her home in the Sierra Nevada foothills of Northern California. Her passion in life is uncovering brilliance in others. Lydia and her team offer mindfulness-based leadership development programs, senior management retreats, and executive coaching. Lydia is a former stockbroker, venture capital project manager, hospice chaplain, and pastor. This unique breadth of experience enables her to transform teams and organizations into engaged, high-performing, fun places to work. She and her husband Jon have five college-age children.

Al Polito has more than 20 years of experience as a business communications professional, helping leaders in technology, manufacturing, utilities, finance, insurance, and real estate navigate their communications challenges with clarity and grace. Deeply committed to helping people through transitions in their personal and professional lives, Al has taught meditative techniques, led mindfulness circles, and facilitated men's support circles in the Portland, Oregon area since 2009. A former touring and recording musician, Al has traveled the world and is now raising a child with his wife, Leah.

Made in the USA
Middletown, DE
03 October 2018